David Mason

Breakout: drive to the Seine

Editor-in-Chief: Barrie Pitt
Art Director: Peter Dunbar

Military Consultant: Sir Basil Liddell Hart
Picture Editor: Robert Hunt

Designer: John Marsh
Cover: Denis Piper
Research Assistant: Yvonne Marsh
Cartographer: Tony Gatrell
Special Drawings: John Batchelor

First printing: May 1969
Printed in United States of America

Ballantine Books Inc.
101 Fifth Avenue, New York, NY10003

Contents

Battle for Normandy

Introduction by Captain Sir Basil Liddell Hart

David Mason's book covers the period from the stalemate in Normandy that developed after the initial success of the Allied landings early in June 1944, through the eventual breakout from that cramped bridgehead at the end of July, to the Allies' triumphant arrival on the Seine and in Paris towards the end of August. He deals ably with the dramatic events of that fateful period, providing a descriptive narrative that holds the reader's attention, and clearly brings out the keypoints of the campaign, blended with an illuminating analysis of the operations – an analysis that is good testimony to the extent and depth of his research.

In view of the many controversial aspects of the period, especially that preceding the breakout, and the rabid partisanship that has been shown in discussing them, it is refreshing to find such a well-balanced treatment of events.

Before the invasion was launched, it could be reckoned that if the Allied armies could gain a bridgehead sufficiently wide and deep to build up their strength on the far side, the French side, of the Channel, the sum of their resources was so much larger than the enemy's that the odds were heavily on a breakout sooner or later. No dam was likely to be strong enough to hold the invading flood in check permanently if the Allies gained enough space to pile up their massed power.

As things turned out, the prolongation of the opening phase, the 'Battle of the Bridgehead', worked out to their advantage. For the bulk of the German forces in the West was drawn there, while arriving in driblets owing to divided views in the German High Command and to constant hindrance from the huge Allied air forces that dominated the sky. The panzer divisions, arriving first and used to fill gaps in the German line, were worn down first – so depriving the enemy of the mobile arm which he needed when it came to fighting in open country. The very toughness of the resistance that so much delayed the Allies' breakout ensured that they would have a clear run through the wide spaces of the French interior, particularly the Loire Valley, once they broke out from Normandy and its hedge-girt 'bocage'.

David Mason's opening chapter deals with the 'Stalemate in Nor-

mandy' that developed in July – accentuated by the summer gales which partly demolished the artificial 'Mulberry' harbours and hampered the build-up. He then turns to the British armoured thrust east of Caen on 18th July named 'Operation Goodwood', which was in itself disappointing – and caused 'storms' behind the scenes – yet, as he emphasises, focussed German attention and resources on that eastern flank. In his next chapter, he comes to 'Operation Cobra', the American offensive on the western flank, launched on 25th July, which culminated in the breakout there. He vividly recounts the driving energy of Patton, whose newly arrived Third Army now took over the 'follow-through'. But he also gives due credit to the key part played by John S Wood, commanding the 4th Armored Division, which was the spearhead of the decisive break-through at Avranches on 31st July as well as of the exploiting drive into Brittany. Moreover, Mason's account likewise brings out the exceptional foresight shown by Wood, in contrast to more conservative-minded superiors, and even Patton, in urging an early wheel eastward instead of wasting time and effort in trying to capture the west coast ports of France, which had become relatively unimportant.

To British readers, David Mason's account may seem to give disproportionate attention to the American part of the campaign – but as it was the Americans who actually achieved the breakout, however much the British contributed indirectly by their pressure and threat on the other flank, his is a proper proportion. It also provides illuminating detail on a side of the campaign about which much less is known.

In subsequent chapters, David Mason deals with Hitler's attempted counterstroke in the west of Normandy (which forfeited the possibility of making an effective stand behind the Seine), with the Canadian attack towards Falaise and its novel methods, with the battle of the 'Falaise pocket', with the Allies' arrival on the Seine, and the liberation of Paris. All of them are interesting, and valuable, for the understanding of events.

Stalemate in Normandy

At the beginning of July 1944, the situation facing the Allies in Normandy was, to say the least, perplexing. A month earlier, on 6th June, they had carried out the greatest amphibious operation in the history of warfare and had gained a toehold on the continent of Europe. Despite the losses, the chaos, and the sheer magnitude of the operation, things had gone as well as might reasonably be expected. Since then, however, the problems had mounted.

Before they could strike out of the landing area, liberate the subjected peoples of western Europe, and drive to the heart of Germany, the Allies faced the task of building upon their invasion achievement by taking control of a substantial area of northern France, and amassing in it sufficient men, munitions, and materials to ensure that once the attack was launched, nothing could bring it to a halt before the Allied forces had reversed the situation in Europe and brought the war in the West to a satisfactory conclusion.

In the month after D-Day, achievements had fallen considerably short of objectives. By the beginning of July, Allied planners had envisaged holding the whole of Normandy, to control twenty-seven airfields on the continent which could accommodate sixty-two squadrons. The reality of the situation was, in the light of those aims, depressing. Only seventeen airfields were in operation, limiting the air power based on the continent to only thirty-one squadrons. Only about one-fifth of the projected area had been taken, and the town of Caen, itself a major objective for D-Day and the vital centre for the approach to the flat plains leading eastwards to the Seine and Paris, remained in German hands. To the west, the Allies were particularly vulnerable in the region of Carentan, a small town straddled across the only road between their troops on the two flanks of the beach-head. The front was only 3½ miles from the coast, and even though a German counterattack in mid-June had been halted 500 yards from the town, there remained the threat that a new concerted effort might split the Allied beach-head in two. Even while the Allies contemplated this possibility, troops using the road and the bridge across the Taute river were subjected to periodic shelling from German artillery positions.

In one of the steady stream of letters which flowed from his pen, General Eisenhower, the supreme commander of the invading forces in Europe, wrote to General Marshall on 5th July 1944 of the toughness of the battle that was taking place in Normandy. He attributed the difficulties to three factors – 'First, as always, the fighting quality of the German soldier; second, the nature of the country; third the weather.'

Eisenhower, in his usual meticulous, sober way, had neither underestimated the difficulties of the fighting, nor misjudged the reasons for them.

There was certainly no underestimating the quality of the German soldier. Even if his generals were coming to the view that the war would be lost and capitulation was the best way out, the individual soldier fought with as much courage as Hitler could have desired. The SS troops and parachute forces who constituted a large proportion of the Seventh Army were an élite who fought with unshakeable tenacity, while the regular Wehrmacht units had almost the same staying power. Only the foreign troops of the German army, the Russians and Poles—who in fact were predominant among the batches of prisoners taken by the Allies—failed to resist with the utmost energy and skill.

Those who did fight well were aided, as Eisenhower had observed, by the Normandy countryside, which was ideal for defence and prevented the effective employment of armour. Most of the Allied advance in the Cotentin Peninsula had to be made through country known as *bocage*, in which the major feature was the hedgerow, a perfect obstacle to tank and infantry alike, and a perfect cover for defending forces. The hedgerow was a tangled mass of brambles and trees up to fifteen feet high, and was firmly based on a solid dirt parapet three or four feet thick and itself up to twelve feet high. These formidable natural obstacles divided the countryside into a patchwork of tiny rectangular fields. Built centuries previously to mark the limits of the fields, and developed as shields to crops, animals and inhabitants against the howling ocean winds, in this month of June 1944 they proved an effective barrier to both man and vehicle. Visibility was limited by the hedgerows to seldom more than 200 to 400 yards. Worse, mobility was curtailed, as the few good roads ran on an axis approximately north-east to south-west, almost exactly perpendicular to the Allies' projected advance to the south-east. The only useable roads were small tracks, often sunken and damp, and overgrown with foliage from the hedgerows to form a dark and uninviting arch. It was perfect country for snipers and for small anti-tank weapons. For the attackers, it proved impossible to manoeuvre artillery, difficult to aim it, and almost impossible anyway to see the enemy at whom it was to be aimed.

As a result of these problems, warfare developed in a style for which the invaders had had virtually no training. In a claustrophobic situation they had to fight forwards in bounds often of only a few yards, with the infantry advancing and the supporting tanks able to follow up only after engineers had blown a way through the base of the hedgerow. The tank commanders found it inadvisable to advance with their heads out of their turrets, since too many comrades had been picked off at short range, and when they stayed inside their vehicles they often had to shake off parties of Germans who swarmed on to the tanks from their concealed positions.

Perhaps the Allied planners were to blame for the selection of this sector for the D-Day landings. Certainly rather less attention seems to have been paid to the countryside that they would have to fight in than to the nature of the beaches across which the landings were to take place. Yet the problems had been considered. Among Allied planners, the argument raged as to whether the countryside would hamper the Allies as they moved forwards after the invasion, or whether it would help the Allies by hindering the Germans' mobility. Perhaps the decisive factor was the probability that the British Second Army, on the left flank of the invasion forces, would make sufficient progress in the region

General Dwight D Eisenhower, Supreme Commander, Allied Expeditionary Force, talks with Major-General Troy Middleton, American VIII Corps Commander. *Above right:* A British patrol, with sten guns and .303 rifles, moves through typical Normandy countryside. *Right:* An early round to the Germans. A Bren gun carrier loaded with ammunition burns after being hit by machine gun fire

The device that foiled the hedgerows: improvised tusks on an American light tank. *Right:* Sergeant Curtis Culin, inventor of the 'rhino' attachment. *Below:* A 'rhino' adapted tank in action

Sherman Hedgecutter
Crew: Five men. *Combat weight:* 30 tons. *Width:* 8 feet 9 inches.
Length: 20 feet. *Maximum speed:* 28 mph (road). *Range:* 80 miles.
Armament: One 75mm gun, two .3 inch machine guns and one
.5 inch machine gun. *Engine:* 460 bhp

of Caen to outflank the difficult terrain of the Cotentin peninsula and advance towards the Seine across the open land of eastern Normandy.

When it became obvious that the advance was in fact going to have to take place through the hedgerow country, the Allies devoted a great deal of energy and ingenuity to devising means of combating the difficulty. Early in July the American 79th Division developed a hedge-cutting device to attach to the front of tanks. Within days other weird and eccentric devices were produced and demonstrated, culminating in an impressive invention attributed to a Sergeant Curtis C. Culin, Jr, of 102nd Cavalry Reconnaissance Squadron. He took the scrap-metal pieces from a knocked-out German road-block, and formed them into a set of prongs that looked like tusks on the front of a tank. When the tank drove these tusks into the base of the hedgerow its front was pinned down, and it could crash through the barrier, instead of over it, without exposing its vulnerable underside to enemy fire, and without pointing its own gun uselessly in the air.

General Bradley inspected the attachment on 14th July, and was so impressed with its performance that he ordered it to be produced *en masse* from scrap metal salvaged from the Germans' own underwater anti-invasion obstacles. For ten days, in preparation for the critical breakout operation, 'Cobra', engineers and ordnance depots worked night and day adapting the tanks. Arc-welding equipment and crews, and some 'tusks' produced in factories, were flown in from England, and by the time Cobra was launched, three out of five tanks engaged in the operation were fitted out in this way. For obvious reasons, the device was known as the 'Rhino' hedgecutter.

While the front line forces in Normandy were dealing with the twin difficulties of the terrain and the tenacity of the enemy, the supporting troops behind them were running up against the third of Eisenhower's difficulties: the weather

On the afternoon of 19th June, to the utter surprise of the meteorologists, a furious gale sprang up in the English Channel and inflicted terrible damage

on Allied equipment, causing severe delays in their programme. Twenty-two sections of a floating roadway intended to relieve the problems of landing supplies over the Normandy beaches were sunk within sight of the harbours. Convoys already in the Channel were sent racing back to port, and as the storm blew on for the next three days, those ships already in position for unloading were subjected to such a buffeting that several dragged their anchors and broke up on the beaches. The artificial 'Mulberry' harbours, towed across the Channel to facilitate the landing of troops and supplies until major ports fell into Allied hands, began to disintegrate. The American Mulberry at St Laurent was a total write-off, and the British one at Arromanches was badly damaged.

When the storm finally died down, over 800 ships were stranded on the beaches, and could be regarded as useless for the purposes of the invasion since they could not be refloated until the next spring tides in July. The storm had succeeded in doing five times more damage to Allied shipping than the opposing forces had managed to inflict on D-Day. Loading was brought to an almost complete halt, the impetus went out of the build-up of stores, and the amount of ammunition and supplies brought in on 20th June – just over 4,500 tons – was only one-fifth of that achieved on 18th June. One immediate result was that General Omar N Bradley, commanding the First U.S. Army, had to restrict the supply of ammunition to most of his troops to one-third of their normal allowance, so that he could adequately equip those immediately concerned in the attack on Cherbourg, which now, in view of the limitations imposed on the landing of supplies by the damage to the Mulberry harbours, took on a new importance. Cherbourg fell soon afterwards on 26th June before

Above right: Storm damage at the Arromanches Mulberry.
Centre right: The attack on Cherbourg; smoke and debris as the Americans blast German positions. *Right:* Cherbourg after the fighting. *Far right:* Major-General Manton S. Eddy, Commander of the 9th Division, which led the assault on Cherbourg

a vigorous attack by General Collins's VII Corps. Even more significantly, it was the dire supply situation which caused the British to postpone the attack across the Odon river which they had planned for 22nd June, when Rommel was left with virtually no reserves and when a concerted push might well have allowed the British Second Army to burst through the Caen/Tilly area, thus freeing the Allies from the stranglehold imposed by the Normandy countryside.

Yet despite the difficulties he had pointed out to Marshall, was Eisenhower right to be so pessimistic? Even if the individual German soldier was fighting back with all the fighting quality his commanders could have wished, did it necessarily follow that the defence was succeeding? The answer may be searched for in two places—first, from the viewpoint of the German commanders responsible for the defence; second, in the pattern of the campaign, and in its adherence to or departure from the agreed plans.

The Germans, despite the need for forces to contain the Soviet armies in the east, and to block the Allied advances in Italy, had amassed powerful forces to oppose the Normandy invaders. Because the Allies elected to land there, it fell to the lot of the German Seventh Army to deal with the invading forces. As part of Army Group B, they were under the command of Field-Marshal Erwin Rommel. Nominally, Rommel was answerable to the C-in-C West, Field-Marshal Gerd von Rundstedt; but in practice, both because of his rank and because of his status in Hitler's eyes, Rommel had direct access to the Führer, with the result that the chain of command was unclear, and a running dispute developed between the two field-marshals. Rommel, anticipating the virtual certainty of Allied air superiority, advocated a static defence, organised with the intention of defeating the invaders on the beaches. Rundstedt, however, proposed a policy of mobile defence, allowing for the movement of reserves from central France to whatever area was currently threatened.

In any case, the dispute never needed to be resolved, for Hitler was by no means content to exercise a purely political function. As German head of state he held the post of Supreme Commander, and he took full advantage of the privilege, refusing to delegate responsibility for the conduct of military affairs to his generals. The course of the war, from a German point of view, remained firmly in Hitler's hands, and while his inspiration and determination had at times weighed heavily in Germany's favour, there were times when his interference made nonsense of the techniques of warfare, and forced his generals both to carry out and to issue orders which they knew to have little or no chance of fulfilment.

Hitler's maniac determination to exercise supreme command was to have important and early consequences, and while the differences between Rommel and Rundstedt remained in force during the battle, events served to dictate the form of the German defence. The Allies refused to be thrown back into the sea as Rommel had hoped, and by maintaining decisive air superiority over Normandy, they also prevented Rundstedt's proposed free movement of reserves, and indeed brought to a halt all daylight traffic within seventy miles of the front.

During the weeks after the invasion, as the Allies doggedly chipped away at the defences to consolidate their beach-head, it was becoming clear to the German commanders that only one defensive policy offered the smallest chance of success, while at the same time they were becoming increasingly pessimistic about the chances of even that policy. By late June it was obvious that the invaders had gone too far to allow the possibility of a counterattack, and there was no alternative but to 'rope off' the Allies, and defend as aggressively as possible, holding them in the beach-head, and denying them room to manoeuvre and to build up their forces and supplies for an attack through France.

But by late June Rundstedt had come to the conclusion that if this were the best they could do, it was pointless to expect any long-term successful outcome. Rommel, too, has accepted that Germany's chance of victory was slim.

The situation was brought to something of a head on 29th June, when Hitler showed his consistent deter-

The defending Commanders, Rundstedt (left) and Rommel

mination to avoid any kind of major withdrawal, however adviseable his generals on the spot felt it to be. On that day, Rundstedt and Rommel went to Berchtesgaden, Hitler's HQ in Bavaria, where Rommel proposed to Hitler that the Seventh Army should fight a rearguard action while withdrawing to the Seine. Rommel had already in late June committed his full reserve in counterattacking a British offensive in the region of the Odon river, and if forced to go on fighting in Normandy Rommel foresaw the early destruction of the entire Seventh Army. Moreover, it was at that stage still anticipated that the Normandy invasion was a feint in order to draw the defences away from the Pas de Calais in preparation for a second, concentrated invasion – the real heart of the Allied attack in the West. And even if he succeeded in holding the Allies within the Normandy beachhead, the call on his reserves would leave no forces with which to reinforce the Fifteenth Army in the Calais area. But Hitler would have nothing to do with the idea. He would certainly countenance no general withdrawal, nor even a limited tactical

re-disposition of forces for a better defence. He was determined not to let the Allies out of the Cotentin peninsula on to the open plains where they could employ their armoured superiority, nor was he prepared to allow morale to be eroded by a withdrawal.

When Rommel and Rundstedt returned to Normandy on 30th June with orders to carry on an aggressive and unyielding defence, they found that the Odon counterattack mounted by the Seventh Army had failed, and its commander, Hausser, obtained from Army Group B headquarters permission for a limited withdrawal in the Caen area.

It appeared that a sensible policy might at last prevail, but when the order was submitted to the Supreme Commander for approval, Hitler, sticking to the policy enunciated on the previous day but not yet transmitted to Hausser, countermanded Army Group B's orders and cancelled the withdrawal. At the end of June and the beginning of July, events moved decisively in the German Army. On 1st July, Hitler reiterated his policy, stating firmly that present positions were to be held, and any further enemy

Left to right: Hausser, Keitel and Kluge

Far left: The ground command in Normandy. Montgomery is flanked by his Army Commanders, Bradley (left) of First US Army, and Dempsey of Second British Army. *Left:* Walter Bedell Smith, SHAEF Chief of Staff.

breakthrough was to be hindered by determined resistance or local counterattack.

That day a final attempt to repulse the Allied attack in the Odon area again came to nothing, and in the evening Rundstedt reported the position to the chief of the armed Forces High Command, the man second only to Hitler in control of the Wehrmacht, Field-Marshal Wilhelm Keitel. Almost wringing his hands in anguish at the news, Keitel repeated the despairing cry 'What shall we do, what shall we do?'

Rundstedt, ever realistic, recommended that they should sue for peace. 'What else can you do?' he asked.

Rundstedt's reward for his realistic outlook was a report to Hitler by Keitel, and a polite letter from the Führer the following day informing him that he had been succeeded by Field-Marshal Günther von Kluge.

If the differences between the German generals and their Supreme Commander were fundamental, there seemed hardly less disagreement among the Allied generals, and the subjects at issue were also twofold: whether the battle was progressing satisfactorily, and whether a breakout from the German ring should be made on the eastern or western flank.

At the centre of the Allies' problem stood the commander of the ground forces in Europe, General Sir Bernard Montgomery. As commander of the 21st Army Group, he had operational control of all the forces in Europe, although General Eisenhower, Supreme Commander of the Allied Expeditionary Force, was to take over this post himself at an appropriate (but unspecified) date in the future. In his 21st Army Group, Montgomery had control of the British Second Army, commanded by Lieutenant-General Sir Miles Dempsey, and the US First Army, commanded by Lieutenant-General Omar N Bradley.

To use his own words, Montgomery's intention was as follows:

'My plan at this stage for developing the break-out operation remained to pin and fight the maximum enemy strength between Villers Bocage and Caen, while the main American thrust swung south and then east to the Le Mans-Alençon area and beyond. In this way I intended to cut the line of withdrawal from Normandy through the Paris-Orleans gap, and so force the Germans back against the Seine below Paris; this would have placed the enemy in a difficult situation as there were no bridges left intact over the river between Paris and the sea.'

And on 11th June 1944, Montgomery had stated: 'My general objective is to pull the Germans onto Second Army so that First Army can extend and expand.'

Yet this scheme, apparently clear in Montgomery's mind, was not so well appreciated by Eisenhower, whose Chief of Staff, Lieutenant-General Walter Bedell Smith, suggested after the event that this plan only developed after the British failed in their first offensive attempt to reach Caen, two weeks after D-Day. At a meeting in April, Montgomery, while not clearly stressing that the task of the Second Army was to stand fast and hold the enemy's main forces in check, envisaged that after the capture of Cherbourg the Second Army would pivot on its left and provide a strong front against enemy movement towards the lodgement area from the east. The British forces would remain in close proximity to their advance bases.

Whether he thought of the plan before the invasion or as a result of the way the enemy forces were building up, it was certainly exactly the antithesis of that envisaged by the early planners, who foresaw a breakout by the British in the open plain to the south-east of Caen, to avoid becoming bogged down in the difficult *bocage* country.

Whichever was the case, the plan as it worked out was in line with Montgomery's professed method of operating. It was always his aim to foresee his enemy's intentions, and use this estimation to outwit his enemy, to manoeuvre him off balance, by making the enemy believe that he was disposing his forces in the right way when in fact he was contributing to his own defeat. Montgomery sought to get inside the mind of his enemies. He had the logic and sense of anticipation of a good chess player. He endeavoured to fight the battle from both sides and ensure that his side had the means to win. For that reason he carried, on the walls of his caravan headquarters, portraits of the opposing generals, and in Normandy in June the images of Rundstedt and Rommel looked down on him as he plotted his strategy.

Whatever the intention of either Montgomery or his colleagues at the time, when the British launched their attack on Caen, it served precisely to fulfil the requirements which Montgomery later outlined. On 28th June the Germans divided their forces in Normandy into two groups to accommodate newly arriving reinforcements. East of Caumont, where they faced mainly the British Second Army, four corps were placed under the control of Panzer Group West. On their left, to the west of Caumont, and facing the US First Army, the German Seventh Army was given control of two corps. German strength on these two sectors, in terms of personnel, was approximately equal, with about 35,000 men each. But the balance of armour and equipment showed exactly the disproportionate attention which Army Group West paid to the two halves of the Allied line. Opposing the British, Panzer Group West had 400 tanks, compared with only seventy-six with which the Seventh Army faced their American opponents. This inequality was further emphasised in other essential weapons, Panzer Group West having a wide margin of advantage over their colleagues in artillery, anti-aircraft guns, and rockets.

The German estimation of Allied plans led them to anticipate an attempted breakout towards Paris in the Caen area. They thought it unlikely that the Americans would mount the major attack in the awkward terrain in which they operated, and in any case in that ideal defensive terrain they felt that the enemy could be held with lighter forces.

In late June and early July, therefore, all aspects of the battle were developing in their predictable directions. The Germans, as Montgomery hoped, were massing at the eastern end of the line, and when the British attacked towards Caen on 25th June it seemed to the Germans that this disposition was vindicated. They counterattacked in force on 29th June, but failed to push the Allies back, and the situation in the Caen region settled down to comparative calm.

While Montgomery had some cause to be pleased that the battle was going the way he intended, his colleagues by no means shared his confidence, and public opinion was turning seriously against him. To those at home, particularly in America, it seemed that while the Americans had taken Cherbourg in a decisive, forceful attack, Dempsey's Second Army had failed to take Caen, and the British had come to a complete standstill. There were those, even, who wondered whether a situation had not already developed akin to that in the First World War when the opposing armies faced each other in a useless, immobile stalemate in a line from the Channel to the Alps.

What was needed, it seemed, to break the deadlock, and bring the battle to life again before the Germans reinforced their defences so strongly that they became wholly impregnable, was some bold, imaginative, unexpected stroke. There was still, after all, the entire Fifteenth Army waiting in the Pas de Calais to beat off the expected second invasion. It could only be a matter of time before the Germans tumbled to the fact that the Normandy landings were the only landings they would have to face, and if the entire strength of the Fifteenth Army were moved into Normandy, the Allies would find themselves in a precarious situation.

While the British appeared to be stalled at Caen, increasing reliance was gradually being placed in General Bradley's launching an attack in the western sector which would break the stalemate and clear the way for the Allies to push on through northern France towards Germany.

In letters written to each other on 25th June, both Montgomery and Eisenhower had agreed on the general advantages of a holding operation against the Germans at the eastern end of the line, while the Americans at the western end attacked to the south.

On 30th June, Montgomery issued his orders to General Bradley, calling for an attack south, pivoting on the left flank in the Caumont area to bring the First US Army into a line facing east. It was proposed to begin the

Bayonet charge, bren gun joining in

German reinforcements move into position. *Opposite page:* An Allied glider has come to grief. *Left:* Unit briefing. *Below:* The infantry hitch a ride. *Bottom:* Camouflage nets are drawn into position

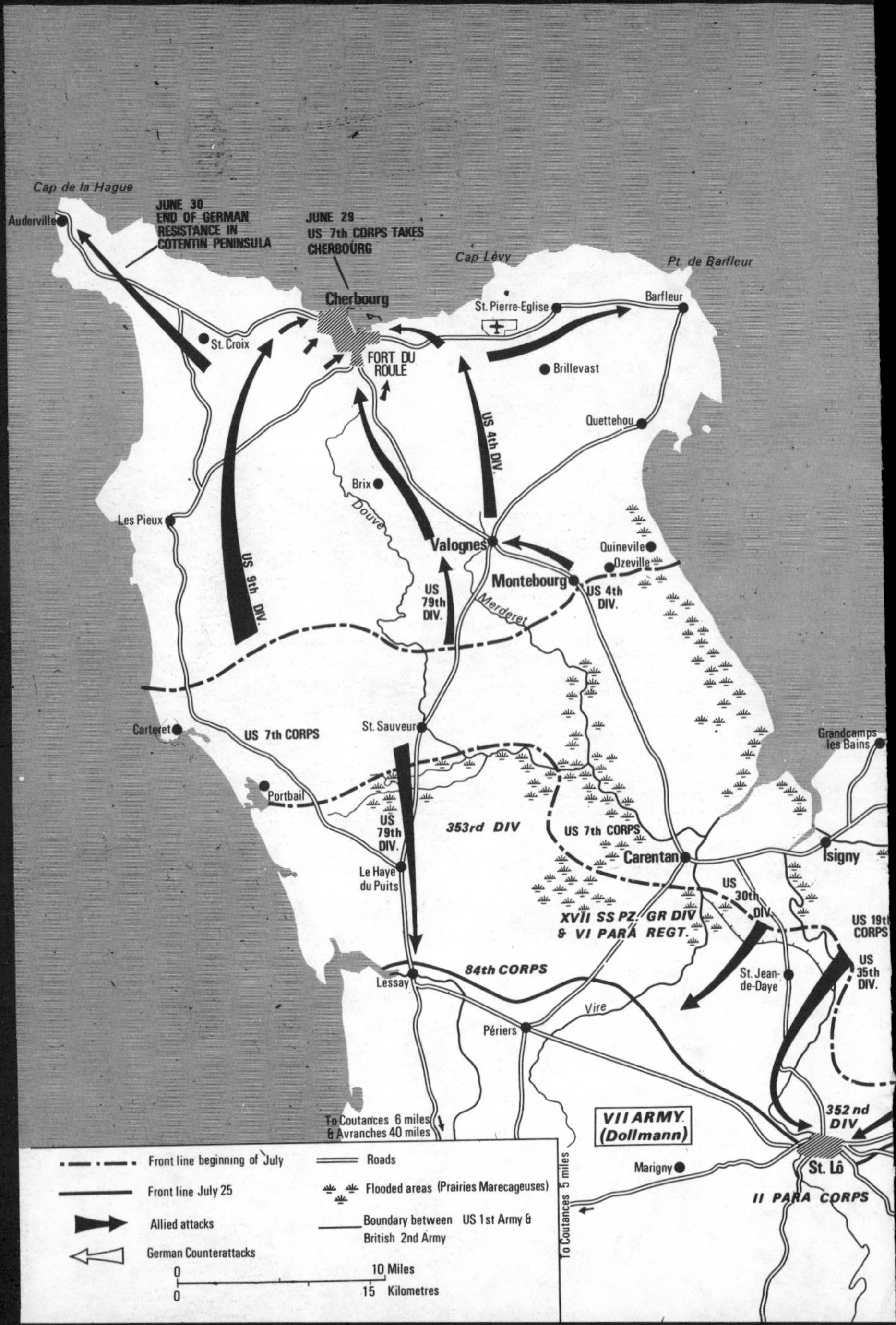

JUNE 30
END OF GERMAN
RESISTANCE IN
COTENTIN PENINSULA

JUNE 29
US 7th CORPS TAKES
CHERBOURG

Cap de la Hague

Auderville

Cap Lévy

Pt. de Barfleur

Cherbourg

St. Pierre-Eglise

Barfleur

St. Croix

FORT DU
ROULE

Brillevast

Quettehou

US 4th DIV

Brix

Quineville
Ozeville

Valognes

Les Pieux

Doure

Montebourg

US 4th
DIV.

US 79th
DIV.

Merderet

US 9th DIV

Carteret

St. Sauveur

US 7th CORPS

Grandcamps
les Bains

Portbail

US 79th
DIV.

353rd DIV

US 7th CORPS

Carentan

Isigny

US
30th
DIV.

US 19th
CORPS

Le Haye
du Puits

XVII SS PZ. GR DIV
& VI PARA REGT.

US
35th
DIV.

Lessay

84th CORPS

St. Jean-
de-Daye

Vire

Périers

To Coutances 6 miles
& Avranches 40 miles

VII ARMY
(Dollmann)

352 nd
DIV

To Coutances 5 miles

Marigny

St. Lô

II PARA CORPS

▬ ▬ ▬ Front line beginning of July	═══ Roads
▬▬▬ Front line July 25	🌿 Flooded areas (Prairies Marecageuses)
◤ Allied attacks	Boundary between US 1st Army & British 2nd Army
◁ German Counterattacks	

0 ———————— 10 Miles
0 ———————— 15 Kilometres

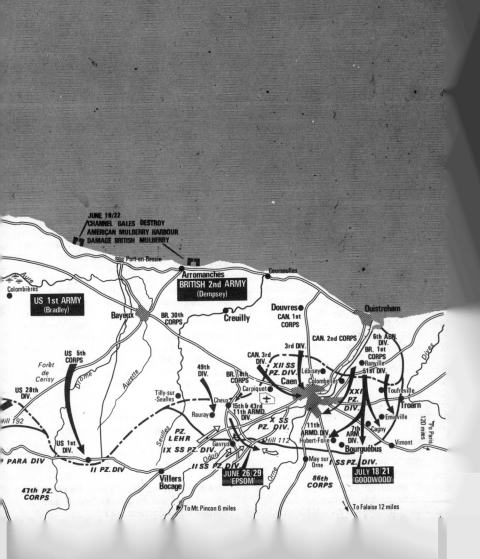

JUNE 19/22
CHANNEL GALES DESTROY
AMERICAN MULBERRY HARBOUR
DAMAGE BRITISH MULBERRY

Port-en-Bessin

Arromanches

Courseulles

BRITISH 2nd ARMY
(Dempsey)

Aure
Colombières

US 1st ARMY
(Bradley)

Bayeux

BR. 30th
CORPS

Creuilly

Douvres

Quistreham

CAN. 1st
CORPS

CAN. 2nd CORPS

6th ABN.
DIV.

US 5th
CORPS

3rd DIV.

Lébisey

Ramville

BR. 1st
CORPS

Drôme

Forêt
de
Cerisy

49th
DIV.

CAN. 3rd
DIV.

XII SS
PZ. DIV.

Caen

Colombelles

51st DIV.

Aurette

BR. 8th
CORPS

Carpiquet

Toufreville

US 28th
DIV.

Tilly-sur-
Sealles

Cheux

15th & 43rd
DIV.
11th ARMD.
DIV.

XXI
PZ.
DIV.

Troarn

Hill 192

US 1st
DIV.

Rauray

X SS
PZ. DIV.

Emieville

Cagny

Vimont

PZ.
LEHR

11th
ARMD.DIV.

7th
ARM.
DIV.

To Paris
120 miles

PARA DIV

IX SS PZ. DIV.

Gavrus

Hill 112

Hubert-Folie

Bourguébus

II PZ. DIV.

II SS PZ. DIV.

Odon

JUNE 26/29
'EPSOM'

May sur
Orne

SS PZ. DIV.

JULY 18/21
'GOODWOOD'

47th PZ.
CORPS

Villers
Bocage

Orne

86th
CORPS

To Mt. Pincon 6 miles

To Falaise 12 miles

Seulles

attack on 3rd July. Bradley planned to carry out these orders by means of a major offensive by his VIII Corps, followed by a development of the offensive by VII and XIX Corps.

The VIII Corps attacked in the area of La Haye du Puits, on the right of the American sector, but encountered firm resistance and by 8th July had progressed only five miles. The VII Corps, attacking down the line of the road from Carentan to Périers, were even more firmly repulsed, and nine days after the attack began it was abandoned. The XIX Corps had some initial success, but by July 10th it too had been virtually halted. It was quickly becoming apparent that a breakout along these lines, on a broad front by all units, was not going to be possible.

To support the American effort, and prevent the Germans moving reinforcements westwards, British Second Army mounted a further attack against Caen. On 4th July Canadian troops under Dempsey's command moved towards the village of Carpiquet, and took it, but they too found it impossible to make further progress. On 7th July a huge bombing attack was laid on by RAF Bomber Command, and as three British and Canadian division followed it up, they were able at last to capture the main part of the city of Caen, although the Germans had withdrawn to the suburbs to the south-east of the city, where they still blocked the way to the open countryside beyond.

These difficulties in the early part of July led to further dissatisfaction. Even the United States War Department was beginning to express its doubts about the prospects of success, and, not surprisingly, Eisenhower's own outlook developed a note of pessimism. On 7th July he wrote to Montgomery voicing concern that the latter, in his efforts to attract the main strength of the German forces onto British Second Army, was concentrating too much on that achievement, and was failing to expand the still limited beach-head, in parts of which, one month after D-Day, the coast was still under fire from German artillery positions. Eisenhower wrote: 'We must use all possible energy to prevent a stalemate, and to insure against fighting a major defensive battle with the

depth we now have.'

Montgomery, however, seemed remarkably undisturbed by the course of events. Far from being disappointed at the lack of decisive progress, he was confident that the tenacity of the enemy's defence was based on inadequate resources. Intelligence estimates and interrogation of captured prisoners were quickly showing that the Germans were pushing their reinforcements into the battle piecemeal, and the heavy casualties involved were, while increasing the apparent ferocity with which the defence was being conducted, only serving to reduce Germany's ability to wage an effective long-term battle. In fact, the root cause of Germany's problem was what Montgomery later termed Hitler's fling at generalship. Having relieved Rundstedt and replaced him with Kluge at the beginning of July, Hitler took a firm control of the battle, and showed a fanatical determination to counter the opinions of those of his generals whom he thought defeatist, that is, any who contemplated a tactical withdrawal of any kind. He sent out a stream of orders demanding that the German troops stand fast, with the result that reinforcements were consumed at a rate which the German Seventh Army could ill afford.

General Bradley was also becoming discouraged about progress. His aim of reaching the Coutances/Caumont line, and thus extricating himself from the hedgerows and occasionally swampy ground in the Cotentin, was still far from being achieved, and on 10th July Bradley reported to Montgomery that he could not contemplate another major offensive until he had both restocked his ammunition supplies and reached firmer ground to the south of the swamps. It was at this time that an idea was beginning to form in Bradley's mind which went against Eisenhower's philosophy of battle, and conformed almost exactly with that of Montgomery's. Having learned from several weeks of slow progress and difficult fighting that a consistent attack on a long line, in this unhelpful terrain and against such determined

The American effort. *Top:* the old ruse aimed at drawing sniper fire. *Right:* A sniper has been located

The advance on Caen

Caen at last. *Top:* Infantrymen of the 1st King's Own Scottish Borderers use a Hotchkiss machine gun against the Germans who remained in Caen.
Centre: British Shermans and 6 pounder anti-tank gun in the town centre.
Bottom: The city that was Caen

defences, was likely to prove fruitless, Bradley began to contemplate a concentrated attack on a narrow front which would smash through the German lines and end the developing stalemate. It could still not be tried until firmer ground had been gained for the massing of his forces, and Bradley estimated that he would need at least another ten days to capture St Lô and reach suitable ground near the St Lô/Pèriers road. It was a delay which Montgomery was well prepared to accept.

It seemed that this might be at last the bold imaginative stroke everybody was hoping for.

It was, however, by no means in line with Eisenhower's view of battle. He, like most other American generals, preferred to build up an overwhelming force and use it in one concerted push along the entire enemy line. If the advance should prove difficult, he was in favour of attempting to resolve it by continually pushing all along the enemy's line until he had stretched it so far that it snapped. Eisenhower was described at one stage as going up and down the line like an American football coach urging everyone to action.

Montgomery, on the other hand, preferred the more subtle approach. His policy, already described, of manoeuvring the enemy off balance, depended mainly on the swift, single, powerful blow, to break the enemy's line in one point, drive on into the rear with all the force he could amass, and prevent the enemy re-forming his line further back. He was in no way concerned to push the Germans gradually back into Germany. He was determined to hold out until he could destroy them in Normandy, and leave the way free for a fast unresisted advance into northern France and on to the enemy's heartland. For that reason he recommended to Bradley that the attack should be confined to a 6,000 yards front.

Bradley appears first to have thought of the idea of a breakthrough on a limited front on 8th July. At their meeting on 10th July he informed Montgomery that he was contemplating the idea, though at that time he had formed no definite plan. Montgomery invited Bradley to take all the time he needed, while the British held the bulk of the German army in the eastern sector. Immediately after that conference, General Dempsey put to Montgomery the idea that the British might launch a strong attack of their own. At first Montgomery was against this plan, since it appeared to contradict his expressed intention of holding the left flank of the bridgehead while the Americans broke through on the right. Soon however, he began to see its attraction, and ordered arrangements to start that day. The plan for this operation, named 'Goodwood', was for a massive stroke by three armoured divisions under VIII Corps, commanded by Lieutenant-General Sir Richard O'Connor, moving in line through the Orne bridgehead behind a powerful aerial bombardment, and fanning out east of the Orne river.

Bradley's attack, also, was to have powerful air support. On 11th July he envisaged that his limited front attack should be preceded by an overwhelming bombardment, and it was hoped that this, combined with a well-timed land operation, would break the German cordon. On 13th July the plan was finalised, given the name 'Cobra', and fixed for July 18th.

In the meantime, the American troops pushed on, and by hard fighting overcame the stubborn opposition and moved south to capture St Lô on 18th July.

On that same day there arose yet another matter of controversy regarding Montgomery's plans. This time, the question was whether Operation Goodwood was to be a further attempt to hold the German forces in the eastern sector, or an attempt at a clean breakthrough, the twin to that contemplated by Bradley for his American forces. The misconception arose from the mention of Falaise in the Operational Instruction on 13th July, which gave the impression that it was to be taken, and from the promise by Montgomery to Eisenhower that the attack would set the Normandy front aflame and achieve a decisive victory. Eisenhower indicated his confidence that the attack would be more than a mere strengthening of the position on the eastern flank, when he foresaw the possibility of a victory that would make some of the old classics look like a skirmish between patrols. But on

On the American front, the battle towards St Lô. *Top:* An American truck is hit by artillery fire. *Centre:* The infantry takes a breather. *Bottom:* For him the war is over, but at least he is alive

15th July Montgomery issued a memorandum to General O'Connor indicating that the main intention of the attack was to write down the German armour, and reiterating the need for a firm bastion on the eastern flank to enable operations of the western flank to continue. Falaise was indeed again mentioned in this memorandum, but only to the extent that the armoured cars were required to push south towards Falaise. It was not specified as an objective.

When, in the following two days, German reinforcements were detected east of the Orne river, General Dempsey ordered O'Connor to establish armoured divisions in the areas Cimont, Garcelles-Secqueville, Hubert Folie and Verrières, thus limiting the objectives to an area several miles short of Falaise, which was barely consistent with the idea of a complete breakout.

Unfortunately, SHAEF (Supreme Headquarters, Allied Expeditionary Forces) still nurtured the impression that Montgomery was contemplating a major breakthrough. Because of organisational and weather problems, the date for Operation Goodwood was finally set at 18th July, and the starting date for Cobra was fixed for 21st July, in order not to divide the air support which each attack needed.

At 0545 hours on the morning of 18th July some 2,100 bombers of Britain's Bomber Command and the US Eighth and Ninth Air Forces dropped delayed-fuse bombs and fragmentation bombs, and at 0745 hours, as the final medium bombers flew away from the scene, the first troops for Operation Goodwood moved off for the ground assault. Led by the 11th Armoured Division attacking south from the Orne bridgehead, they made good initial progress, and by midday had reached the area of Tilly la Campagne. Then, however, they ran into a most determined opposition, particularly from German 88mm guns and Panther tanks. While the bombing had worked to the extent that prisoners were too stunned to be interrogated for 24 hours, it had not been deep enough. In the first layer of defence the tanks encountered little opposition, but further on, particularly in the region of Cagny, the defences had survived the bombing, and they inflicted heavy damage on the attacking troops. The 11th Armoured Division lost 126 tanks that day, and Guards Armoured Division, operating on their left, a further sixty.

That night the Germans withdrew from the eastern suburbs of Caen, and took up positions on the already well-defended Bourguebus Ridge, south of Caen, where their guns occupied commanding positions overlooking VIII Corps' projected line of advance. On 19th and 20th July the attacks continued, but the enemy rushed reserves into position from west of the Orne river and from the Caumont sector, and the advance gradually slowed down until, on the afternoon of 20th July, a storm broke over the battlefield which turned the dry and dusty ground into a sea of mud across which further progress was impossible.

The Allies had secured a new line, reaching as far south as Tilly la Campagne and as far east as Troarn, and had cleared the defenders out of the important Caen bottleneck. But there had been no breakout in the east. And it was this which once more blackened Montgomery's reputation at SHAEF headquarters and threw Eisenhower again into a mood of despondency. Yet Montgomery remained sublimely confident, and was perfectly happy to welcome both Eisenhower and Churchill on visits to Normandy.

Even as the storms were breaking over the battlefield, he indicated to a somewhat surprised Eisenhower that he was perfectly happy about the way the battle was going, and when Churchill flew in on 21st July he was soon persuaded that the battle was going according to plan, and that a major victory was imminent. On his return, though, Churchill was unable to dispel all the doubts about Montgomery's success.

On the same day, 21st July, Eisenhower showed exactly how perturbed he was by writing to Montgomery, asking whether they saw eye-to-eye on big problems. He appeared to be unhappy about the share of the effort the Allies were taking, and suggested that although the United States armies would eventually outnumber the British, 'while we have equality in size we must go forward shoulder to shoulder, with honors and sacrifices

In the air Allies held supremacy

equally shared.' He pointed out that he had been extremely hopeful and optimistic that Goodwood, assisted by a tremendous air attack, would have a decisive effect on the battle of Normandy. Since that had not come about, he was pinning his immediate hopes on Bradley's attack.

Montgomery replied that he had no intention of stopping offensive operations on the eastern flank. He had already, on the day Eisenhower wrote, ordered Dempsey to continue intensive infantry operations to make the enemy believe that they were still about to attempt an advance towards Falaise. He did, however, make a further attempt to meet the terms of the letter by urging Dempsey on with more specific instructions.

Yet was Eisenhower right to worry? Despite all the intelligence estimates and interrogations of enemy prisoners, he had, of course no way of knowing the exact enemy dispositions, but it nevertheless became apparent later that Montgomery, even though he had failed to achieve all the tactical objectives for the battle, had succeeded within the terms of his overall strategy by holding the Germans in the east to facilitate progress in the west. As a direct result of the Goodwood operation, two German divisions were deployed against the British which would otherwise have had a marked effect on Operation Cobra: 2nd Panzer Division was pulled to the south of Caen from the Caumont area, instead of going into reserve, and 116th Panzer Division was diverted there instead of being sent to the area south of St Lô, where it would have been almost precisely in the path of the planned American breakout. In addition part of 9th SS Panzer Division was moved to the Caen area before it had completed a refit.

On the eve of its breakout, therefore, the American First Army faced only nine divisions, including two Panzer divisions and one Panzer Grenadier division, which itself was only lightly armoured with a battalion of assault-guns. Contrasted with the fourteen divisions, including seven Panzer divisions and four heavy tank battalions which defended the Caen/Falaise plain on the Second Army front, it seems that the strategy Montgomery had

assiduously pursued was being vindicated.

In addition to the matter of troops dispositions, a number of other factors had been working, indirectly, to influence the course of the battle. To the soldiers closely concerned in the fighting, who knew only the fury and determination with which the troops in the German front line defended their positions, it was perhaps not easily apparent. But the more perceptive commanders could appreciate that wars, unlike battles, are won by the armies with the deepest resources, that critical aspects of the fighting might be taking place miles from the actual front, and that a temporary tactical setback is not necessarily an accurate indication of the strategic position. Thus it was in the Battle of Normandy. While the British were making slow progress in the area of Caen, and the Americans were bogged down in the hedgerow country of the Cotentin, the Allied air forces were having a decisive effect on the enemy's capacity to resist the invading forces.

They had already wrecked all the bridges over the Seine below Paris, and those over the Loire below Orleans, and they had started a systematic destruction of the lines of communication in the Paris/Orleans gap, to cut the only remaining route through which reinforcements and supplies could reach the Normandy battlefield. By mid-June they had reduced the number of usable railways to two, and the roads were severed by craters and broken bridges. Moreover, in addition to a virtually continuous attack on transport through the gap during daylight, which brought traffic to a complete halt, they also lit the target areas with flares for night attacks, so that transport could seldom move more than twenty miles per day even under cover of darkness.

Equally serious for the Germans, in the long run, was the effect on fuel supplies which had proved in the preceding years of the war to be the vital element in the success or failure of so many campaigns. At the time when the destruction of the railways was imposing heavier burdens than ever on the roads, the US Eighth Air Force was stepping up its offensive against the synthetic oil plants which supplied

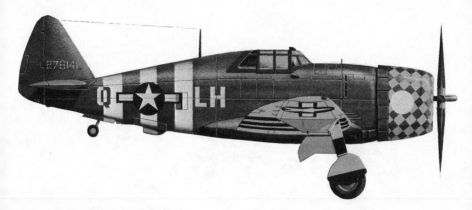

Republic P-47D Thunderbolt
Engine: Pratt & Whitney R-2800-59, 2,300 hp. *Armament:* 6 or 8 .5 inch
Browning machine guns with 300-425 rounds per gun plus two 1,000 pound
and one 500 pound bombs or 6 or 10 rockets. *Maximum speed:* 429 mph at
30,000 feet. *Initial climb rate:* 2,780 feet per minute. *Ceiling:* 42,000 feet.
Weight empty: 10,000 pounds. *Weight loaded:* 14,500 pounds.
Span: 40 feet 9 inches. *Length:* 36 feet 1 inch

almost all the Luftwaffe's fuel. In May
the refineries at Leuna and Politz had
been put out of production, and in
June that at Schölven was destroyed.
The effect was a reduction in the out-
put of fuel from 5,850 tons per day
during April, to 2,800 tons per day
during May, to only about 1,750 tons
per day during June.

Albert Speer, Germany's talented
and energetic Minister of Armaments
and War Production, felt compelled to
warn Hitler of the gravity of the
situation. On 30th June he wrote: 'If
we do not succeed in protecting the
synthetic plants and refineries better
than in the past, then an unbridgeable
gap will appear in the fuel supply of the
Armed Forces and the homeland... By
September it will no longer be possible
to cover the most urgent of the necessary supplies for the Wehrmacht.'

But by now there had begun an inescapable spiral. Because of the in-
effectiveness of the Luftwaffe, the
Allied air forces had been unimpeded
in their activities over Europe. They
had destroyed the fuel sources which
supplied the Luftwaffe, which led
immediately to economies in aircraft
activities. Inevitably the first to suffer
were those at the end of the supply
line, in Normandy, and one of the first
measures was the retention in Ger-

many of eight groups of fighters, each
consisting of about thirty-five aircraft, which were due to return to
Normandy after refitting. The reduction of fighter reinforcements consequently led to even greater freedom
for the Allied bombers to range freely
over northern Europe, searching for
targets and attacking them at will.

The resulting Allied air domination
over the Normandy battlefield prevented even the available reinforcements
arriving at the right time. In the fierce
fighting between the invasion and the
eve of the Cobra operation, the two
armies located to deal with the Allies,
Panzer Group West and the Seventh
Army, had suffered nearly 117,000
casualties, but less than 12,000 men
had arrived to replace them. They had
similarly been able to replace only
seventeen of their 250 tank losses. Significantly, these problems were the
result almost entirely of the disrup-
tion to communications. There had
been no failure on the part of industry,
for German fighter and tank production both reached wartime peaks during the early summer of 1944, with the
production of 4,545 fighters during
April, May and June, and 2,313 tanks
during the three months up to the end
of July. A further contributory factor,
even more remote from the main-

Above: Winston Churchill visits the front near Caen and talks with General Simonds (with map) and Generals Montgomery and Dempsey. Left: The Germans have a group of Allied soldiers pinned down in a wood in the Orne river sector

stream of the battle but an equally important link in the endless chain which makes up an efficient fighting force, was the drain on manpower resources. As its losses grew, the Luftwaffe was compelled to man its fighters with instructors from the training schools, which meant not only a deterioration in the quality of the fighter pilots, but promised further inevitable shortages of trained pilots at a later stage.

Most important of all was Hitler's unyielding determination to stand fast, and permit only limited withdrawal from hedgerow to hedgerow, which necessarily involved throwing troops incessantly into the firing line, where they met their early destruction. It has been generally agreed since that the only reasonable course for Hitler to take at that stage was a strategic withdrawal to the Seine, where they could defend a natural obstacle which the Allies themselves would find difficult to cross partly on account of their own recent bombing activity.

Taken together, this multiplicity of factors meant that when they were eventually able to contemplate a breakout, the advantage lay substantially with the Allies. Montgomery, with his unshaken confidence that the plan was working out, appeared to know this. And even if his view was shared by too few of his Allied colleagues, it was still being constantly confirmed, as the build-up progressed, by the enemy commanders.

As early as 15th July, two days before he was severely injured in a road crash when Allied aircraft strafed his staff car, Rommel reported to Kluge, the new C-in-C West: 'Within a measureable time, the enemy will succeed in breaking through our thinly held front, especially that of Seventh Army, and in thrusting deep into France . . . The force is fighting heroically everywhere, but the unequal struggle is nearing its end. In my opinion, it is necessary to draw the appropriate conclusion from this situation.'

Kluge himself became even more despondent. On 21st July he wrote to Hitler a letter which merits examination in full:

'My discussion yesterday with the commanders in the Caen sector has afforded regrettable evidence that, in face of the enemy's complete command in the air, there is no possibility of our finding a strategy which will counter-balance its truly annihilating effect, unless we give up the field of battle.'

'Whole armoured formations, allotted to the counterattack, were caught in bomb-carpets of the greatest intensity, so that they could be extricated from the torn-up ground only by prolonged effort and in some cases only by dragging them out. The result was that they arrived too late. The psychological effect of such a mass of bombs coming down with all the power of elemental nature upon the fighting troops, especially the infantry, is a factor which has to be given particularly serious consideration. It is immaterial whether such a bomb-carpet catches good troops or bad: they are more or less annihilated. If this occurs frequently, then the power of endurance of the forces is put to the highest test; indeed, it becomes dormant and dies.'

'I came here with the fixed determination of making effective your order to stand fast at any price. But when one has to see by experience that this price must be paid in the slow but sure annihilation of the force . . . anxiety about the immediate future of this front is only too well justified . . . In spite of intense efforts, the moment has drawn near when this front, already so heavily strained, will break. And once the enemy is in open country, an orderly command will hardly be practicable in view of the insufficient mobility of our troops. I consider it my duty to bring these conclusions to your notice, my Führer, in good time.'

As an analysis of the situation and an indication of what might be expected in the near future, Kluge's letter could hardly be bettered. What he did not know at the time he wrote it was that within three days another 'mass of bombs' was due to come down 'with all the power of elemental nature' upon the fighting troops. And the consequences were to be momentous.

Cobra strikes

When General Bradley outlined his plans for Cobra at a conference of his corps commanders on 12th July, he seemed determined to make the operation a success, almost at any cost. He called for aggressive action, and said that severe losses might have to be borne. But, he warned, the alternative was not attractive: 'If they (the enemy) get set again, we shall go right back to this hedge fighting and you can't make any speed.' His final word was typical of the American attitude which seemed to characterise this campaign: 'This thing must be bold.'

On 19th July General Bradley flew to England to outline his requirements for the air bombardment. The target area was a rectangle just to the south of the road between Périers and St Lô, 7,000 yards wide and 2,500 yards deep. The requirements for the bombing posed several problems, and led eventually to a number of uneasy compromises. Bradley wanted a massive air bombardment, designed to fulfil the artillery's normal role of disrupting communications and creating material and moral havoc among the enemy. He asked that the bombing should be

carried out over a short time for maximum blast effect, but he asked that only light bombs should be used, to avoid the excessive cratering which had hampered tank mobility in Operation Goodwood. To ensure a quick follow-up, Bradley proposed to withdraw his forces only 800 yards from the start line, and to make certain that no bombs fell on his own troops, he requested that the bomb runs be made across the field of battle, parallel to, rather than perpendicular to, the start line.

But the air chiefs disagreed. They insisted on a bomb run from north to south, to avoid German anti-aircraft interference which they thought would inevitably accompany long runs over enemy-held territory. Bradley argued that they could use the sun for concealment from ground anti-aircraft units, flying from the east if they attacked during the morning, and from the west if they attacked in the afternoon. He also pointed out that the pilots could use the road as a landmark, keeping to the south of it to avoid accidentally bombing American troops. The air chiefs argued, in turn,

Plotting the breakout. In a field near St Lô Montgomery discusses the air strike with Dempsey and Air Vice-Marshal Sir Trafford Leigh-Mallory (right), Commander-in-Chief of the Allied Expeditionary Air Forces

that the road would serve equally well as a landmark on runs over the heads of the ground troops, by indicating a clear line which the pilots must cross before bombing.

The north-south bomb runs appear to have been settled in the minds of the air chiefs, who understood that Bradley was prepared to accept casualties among his troops, but Bradley seems to have gone away with the impression that lateral runs would be used. In his book, *A Soldier's Story* he writes: 'Had I known of air's intent to chance the perpendicular approach, I would never have consented to its plan.'

The air chiefs also insisted on a greater margin of safety than 800 yards. They wanted 3,000 yards, but in order to allow Bradley to move his troops into the bombed areas without delay, they agreed to reduce this to 1,500 yards. Bradley refused to withdraw more than 1,000, then he extended this to 1,200 yards. Reducing their own demand from 1,500 to 1,450, the air chiefs agreed to make up the difference by forbidding heavy bombers within 250 yards of the road, and only allowing

the more accurate fighter-bombers to operate in the area.

Finally, the intensity of the bombing was agreed: 2,500 planes were to take part, dropping 5,000 tons of high explosives, white phosphorous, and napalm on the target.

The main breakthrough effort was to be made by General Collins's VII Corps. Following the air bombardment, 9th and 30th Infantry Divisions and part of the 4th Infantry Division were to make the initial penetration and secure the flanks of the breach, creating a 'defended corridor'. Through this corridor the armour would come into action. The 1st Infantry Division, motorised for the operation, with part of 3rd Armoured Division, was to stream through and attack towards Coutances, while the remainder of 3rd Armoured Division was to make a wider sweep towards Coutances, and 2nd Armoured Division an even wider movement as far to the south-east as Tessy-sur-Vire and to the south-west as Cérences.

The attack was planned to start on 20th July, but bad weather caused its postponement from day to day until

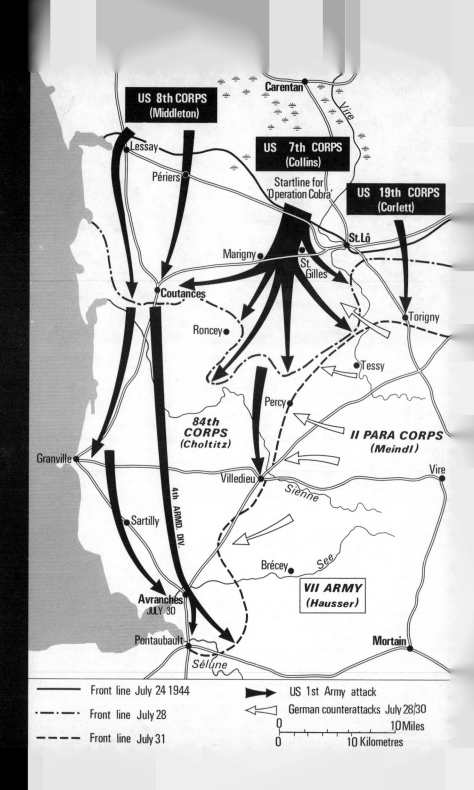

US 8th CORPS (Middleton)

US 7th CORPS (Collins)

Startline for 'Operation Cobra'

US 19th CORPS (Corlett)

Carentan

Vire

Lessay

Périers

St.Lô

Marigny

St. Gilles

Coutances

Roncey

Torigny

Tessy

Percy

84th CORPS (Choltitz)

II PARA CORPS (Meindl)

Granville

Vire

Villedieu

Sienne

4th ARMD. DIV.

Sartilly

Brécey

See

VII ARMY (Hausser)

Avranches JULY 30

Pontaubault

Mortain

Sé025lune

	Front line July 24 1944		US 1st Army attack
—·—·—	Front line July 28	◁	German counterattacks July 28/30
— — —	Front line July 31		

0 ————— 10 Miles

0 ————— 10 Kilometres

24th July, when Air Chief-Marshal Sir Trafford Leigh-Mallory, commander of the Allied Expeditionary Air Force, at last gave the signal that unleashed the mighty air bombardment. Flying out over France himself, Leigh-Mallory then promptly found conditions unsuitable for the air attack with the sky overcast and visibility poor, and he ordered it to be called off.

Unfortunately, his signal reached base in time to cancel only part of the bombing programme, and more than 300 bombers went ahead with their assignments. The result was tragic. Some of the bombs were accidentally released short of the start line; twenty-five American soldiers were killed and 131 others wounded. The premature bombing also had the unfortunate effect of alerting the Germans to the probability of an attack, and Bradley was left wondering whether the Americans had sacrificed tactical surprise, and whether the attack should be postponed for several days while a new pattern of air support was devised. But the problem was quickly resolved, if not solved. His superiors wanted action, there was no time for delay, and a fresh start was ordered for 1100 hrs on the morning of 25th July.

On that day the bombing was devastating. More than 1,500 B-17 and B-24 heavy bombers dropped 3,300 tons of explosives in the target area; more than 380 medium bombers came over and released fragmentation bombs; and more than 550 fighter-bombers dropped 200 tons of bombs and napalm. And nobody escaped their terrifying onslaught, not the Germans, nor the French civilian population, nor – once again – the American soldiers waiting to follow up.

Kluge, after the bombing of the 24th, had anticipated an intensive attack, and had told Hausser, the Seventh Army Commander: 'Without any doubt, there is something new in all this air activity. We have got to expect a heavy enemy offensive somewhere.' Accordingly Lieutenant-General Fritz Bayerlein, commander of the Panzer Lehr Division, had deployed his tanks in the natural cover of the sunken lanes, where he hoped they would be protected by the hedgerows. The cover was far from adequate, as Bayerlein later related: 'The planes kept coming over, as if on a conveyor belt, and the bomb carpets unrolled in great rectangles. My flak had hardly opened its mouth, when the batteries received direct hits which knocked out half the guns and silenced the rest. After an hour I had no communication with anybody, even by radio. By noon nothing was visible but dust and smoke. My front lines looked like the face of the moon and at least seventy per cent of my troops were out of action – dead, wounded, crazed or numbed. All my forward tanks were knocked out, and the roads were practically impassable.'

But the cloud of dust thrown up by the bombing drifted to the north, and the boundaries of the target area became obscured. Again some bombs fell short of the target area, killing 111 more soldiers, including the commander of the United States Army Ground Forces, General Lesley J. McNair, and wounding another 490. An American company commander described in graphic terms the effect of the bombardment: 'The dive-bombers came in beautifully and dropped their bombs right where they belonged. Then the first group of heavies dropped them several hundred yards in front of us. The next wave came in close, the next one still closer. The dust cloud was drifting back towards us. Then they came right on top of us. The shock was awful. A lot of the men were sitting around after the bombing in a complete daze. I called battalion and told them I was in no condiion to move, that everything was completely disorganised and it would take me some time to get my men back together, and asked for a delay. But battalion said no, push off. Jump off immediately.'

Despite the mistake, the ground attack went off with only a slight delay, but the troops immediately ran into further disappointment. Most of them expected the bombing to have demolished the Germans sufficiently for them to cross the road and walk on unopposed. They were understandably shaken when they found that in patches where the bombs had not fallen the Germans were able to poke their heads out of their foxholes and defend with as much determination as ever. The result was that at the end of the

The attempt to gain firm open ground for the breakout cost heavy casualties. *Top left:* Airborne Troops, fighting to clear the bocage country on the coastal flank, suffered badly. These were wounded and taken prisoner. *Top right:* The debris of battle. *Above:* The road to St Lô. *Left:* Lieutenant General Lesley J McNair, Chief of Army ground forces, killed accidentally in the breakout bombardment. *Opposite page:* The hedgerow country

The Americans gain ground

day, the three American divisions in the initial attack had only just managed to get across the Périers/St Lô road, and there was no sign yet of any penetration of the German lines.

Indeed, General Collins was faced with a delicate decision. He could find no signs of an organised defence, but was uncertain what this meant. Had the German lines been smashed? Or had they been warned by the mistaken bombing of 24th July, and withdrawn to reform beyond the limits of the bombed area? Should Collins therefore commit his armour, and ram home the effect of the attack even though his infantry had still not achieved their objectives? Or would his tanks be met with a counterattack or an ambush, and left in a congested and vulnerable position? Collins decided to gamble, and commit his tanks the following morning. While Collins was deliberating on the use of armour, Kluge, by the evening of 25th July, had already reached an accurate appreciation of the position, and he admitted: 'As of this moment, the front has burst.'

And one shrewd intelligence officer attached to VII Corps in fact agreed with him, having already guessed that the German line was now stretched so thin that 'there was nothing in back to stop us.'

The armoured thrusts that were to clarify the entire picture went in soon after daybreak on 26th July. The 1st Infantry Division, with Combat Command B of the 3rd Armoured Division, under Major-General Clarence R Huebner, attacked towards Marigny, aiming to capture the town quickly and push on towards Coutances. At the same time Major-General Edward H Brookes, commanding 2nd Armoured Division on the left flank, was planning to take St Gilles.

Huebner's 1st Infantry Division made only moderate progress. Units of the German 353rd Division and 2nd SS Panzer Division fought with their usual ferocity and even with the help of artillery, tank fire, and an aircraft strike the Americans were still a mile from Marigny after two days, and there was no sign of being able to exploit towards Coutances.

On the left flank, however, affairs were taking a very different course. Brookes's spearhead was being led by

Combat Command A, under Brigadier-General Maurice Rose, with 22nd Infantry attached. And after the tough and bloody slogging of the past weeks it suddenly seemed remarkably easy. One tank was destroyed immediately after crossing the Périers/St Lô road, but from then on there was no more than sporadic opposition. That afternoon Combat Command A found themselves through St Gilles and moving steadily south along the road to Canisy. There was indeed 'nothing in back' to stop them; the defence seemed to have evaporated – and VII Corps had broken through.

The following day, 27th July, brought confirmation of the good news. On the right flank of the breakthrough, 9th Division pushed south and west, while in the centre 4th Division raced forward almost to Carantilly. On the left flank, 30th Division pushed west to the outskirts of St Lô, and south for six miles along the bank of the Vire river, almost without opposition. General Leland S Hobbs, 30th Division commander, was jubilant, and may be forgiven if he confused his metaphors when shortly before midnight on 27th July he exclaimed: 'This thing has busted wide open. We may be the spearhead that broke the camel's back.'

Throughout the night on 26th July and all day on the 27th, the Allied armoured thrusts were ranging south to roll back the scant opposition. General Rose's Combat Command A split into a three-pronged attack, took le Mesnil-Herman and le Mesnil-Opac, and secured the nearby high ground (designated Hill 183) which commanded the important road network in the area.

The men of Combat Command B, under Colonel Truman E Boudinot, were having a more difficult time. Their aim was to capture high ground in the region of the road between St Lô and Coutances, which itself would form the axis of his advance and provide a fast way through the *bocage* to Coutances itself. If they succeeded, their achievement would have far-reaching results, in cutting off the retreat of the German forces still facing VII Corps, and trapping them in the triangle formed by the coast and the two roads St Lô/Lessay, and St Lô/

Top: Americans roll into St Lô
Above: The town lies in ruins.
Right: Captured German anti-tank gun

Top: Americans rest under cover on the way up

Prisoners of war

Coutances. At first they had difficulty passing through Marigny, and throughout the day, except on the road itself where the opposition was slight, they were harassed by pockets of fierce resistance in the hedgerows. Moreover, the Germans had reacted to the news that Americans had broken through, and were already drawing up a hasty defensive line facing east, to prevent being isolated with their back to the coast. While 2nd SS Panzer Division held back Combat Command B in its push towards Coutances, almost all the units of LXXXIV Corps were able to move either through the elongated American columns or around the western end of their spearhead.

Kluge had been slow to react to the threat from VII Corps in Normandy, and on the critical day, 27th July, as a direct result of Montgomery's policy of keeping the Germans off balance, he had been out of the important sector inspecting defensive positions near Caen. But Hitler was even slower. It seems astonishing that, even though the Germans knew they lacked defence in depth, they only now began to move reinforcements from the south of France, where they waited for another Allied invasion. On 28th July Hitler ordered the 84th, 331st, and 708th Infantry Divisions, and the 9th Panzer Division, to start the journey north.

With the German forces pouring to

the south, and VII Corps pursuing its drive to the west, the map had by the night of 28th July been completely redrawn. Instead of the enemy trapped in the triangle, the remnants of the German defence had formed a new front line a couple of miles south of the road from Brehal to Tessy-sur-Vire, and nearly ten miles south of Coutances.

But the withdrawal was not without incident, and several bitter actions took place which cost the Germans heavily. On the afternoon of 29th July, Allied aircraft spotted a line of German vehicles held up in a solid traffic jam on the road near Roncey. For six hours the planes tore into the target, and with no way of driving out of the jam, the Germans were given the unhappy choice of sitting in their vehicles and being shot up, or taking to the fields on foot. Not unnaturally, they took to their heels and fled, and at the end of the day the road was even more inextricably blocked with the unmanned wrecks of more than one hundred tanks and over 250 other vehicles.

Of the Germans who escaped, many were captured during the night or on the following morning, and several units gave themselves up wholesale, after displaying a brief token resistance as a gesture to their military honour. Among the more spirited German counterattacks was one launched from the south by defending forces, and from the north by the escapers, against American outposts in the vicinity of St Denis le Gast. Nearly 1,000 Germans attacked with one hundred armoured vehicles, and the Americans were almost put to flight. Had the Germans been tenacious enough to follow up their initial success, they might well have halted Combat Command B's advance and possibly even contained the breakout altogether. But by now morale had drained away, and the Germans were more interested in survival than in well organised countermeasures. The attack eventually petered out, and when the Germans resumed their flight, they left behind 130 dead and 124 wounded, together with 500 prisoners, seven captured tanks, and a score of other vehicles.

Later that night another column of Germans, in eleven vehicles, moved unchallenged into the American lines near Lengronne. When eventually they were stopped, they were well into an American artillery bivouac area, and both sides, apparently astonished to discover the enemy so close, opened fire at point-blank range. The quiet night erupted in a spontaneous inferno of shot and shell, noise and flame. Machine-guns, rifles, howitzers, even tank shells were poured into the eleven vehicles and their hapless crews. Before long the Germans stopped returning the fire, and the skirmish quietened again. The morning revealed ninety dead against the Americans' five, and there were 200 prisoners.

In another battle more than 200 Germans set out to break through the lines of the 41st Armoured Infantry. They almost overran the Americans, until a sergeant of 41st Armoured Infantry, acting with the cool initiative which so often turns a battle, jumped on to a tank, shouted orders to its crew, and with well-directed close range fire took the impetus out of the German advance. The Americans pulled themselves together, directed artillery fire at their enemy, and put them into confusion. About a hundred prisoners were taken, and 450 Germans were killed, against losses of fifty American troops killed and sixty wounded.

It had been a hot night for those units caught in the fighting, and the cold dawn broke to reveal the litter of dead Germans and broken vehicles. Throughout that morning, 30th July, the sounds of sporadic outbursts of fire were heard within the American lines, as Combat Command B hunted down and either captured or killed those Germans who had not succeeded in escaping during the night. At noon a hundred Germans walked into the American command post and gave themselves up, and the fighting was over.

Without doubt the main force of the German defence had escaped. As one officer of the American 1st Division put it, 'the big fish had been lost in the trap.' The 'big fish' which escaped consisted mainly of the 2nd SS Panzer Divisions, 17th SS Engineer Battalion, 17th SS Panzer Grenadiers, and 6th Parachute Regiment.

Breakthrough

With the breakthrough now a fact, the Allies faced possibly the most critical phase in the entire campaign, a phase which depended on quick and far-reaching decisions. The landing in Normandy had been planned to the finest detail, and had been accomplished broadly according to plan. Since then, the weeks of exhausting and costly fighting as the bridgehead was expanded served to dispel the post-D-Day optimism and inject despondency into the atmosphere. Now, with the breakthrough accomplished, the entire future seemed to be opening up again. If the Allies seized their chance, there was every prospect of destroying the German army in the West. If they faltered now, with no other opportunity clearly apparent, history would harshly judge the Allied leaders for their failure.

At one time Bradley had anticipated a 'holding and mopping up' operation after the breakout. Now he faced a choice, either of pausing to consolidate, or of maintaining the momentum and keeping the Germans reeling back in disarray, allowing them no time to re-establish their defences. In the circumstances, the answer was so clear that there was really no choice at all. And on 28th July Bradley issued orders to First Army for the immediate implementation of Montgomery's broad plan: to drive on without pause beyond Avranches and Mortain, swing up to the line Caumont Fougères, then make a wide sweep south of the *bocage* country to the Le Mans/Alençon line, in preparation for the drive east against the Germans. All thought of consolidation was jettisoned. The VII and VIII Corps were to continue the exploitation south.

At the same time, to avoid the problems which inevitably accrue from a single spectacular success on a narrow front, Bradley issued orders to the other two corps of First Army aimed at keeping the front line in balance.

In the centre of the American front, XIX Corps, commanded by Major-General Charles H Corlett, was to attack south towards a loosely-defined objective which included the town of Vire and the Forêt de St Sevel. This attack had several aims: it would prevent the Germans using either the town or the high ground in that area

Montgomery with his American commanders. Left to right, Major-General Walter Robertson, 2nd Infantry Division, Major-General Leonard Gerow, V corps Major-General Edward Brooks, 2nd Armoured Division, and Major-General Clarence Huebner, 1st Division. *Far-right:* Lieutenant-General Courtney Hodges, Deputy Commander and later Commander of First US Army

as a pivot on which to form a coherent withdrawal; it also had the prospect of providing First Army itself with a pivot on which to carry out its swing into line facing to the east for the advance to the Seine; and not least from a military and psychological point of view, it would get the Americans at last out of the Cotentin peninsula, and the *bocage* country, and leave the gruelling fighting of the hedgerows far behind.

On XIX Corp's left flank, V Corps had a comparatively free objective, to pursue the enemy as hard as possible, and, as their commander, General Gerow, told his men, 'not give the Boche a chance to dig in.'

The most sensational advance, as might be expected, was in the coastal area of the Cotentin, where the defences had consistently been shown to be weakest throughout the campaign, and where VII Corps had already set in motion a general panic among the Germans defending the sector. And as the exploitation got under way, changes were becoming effective in the American command. For the prospective move into Brittany, Third Army was to become operational, under the command of General Patton, and would include VIII Corps. General Bradley himself would at that stage take over command of 12th Army Group, with Lieutenant-General Courtney H Hodges, until then his deputy commander in First Army, promoted to its command. Clearly, if the current rate of progress was maintained, the moment for the changeover to the new command structure was not far off, and to prepare for it, Bradley asked Patton, informally and temporarily, to supervise the activities of VIII Corps on the coastal flank. The arrangement would establish a useful continuity between the exploitation of the Cobra breakthrough and the operation in Brittany.

Immediately he took over, even in his limited supervisory role, Patton began to impose his own style on the attack. He withdrew his infantry spearheads and replaced them with two armoured divisions, 4th Armoured commanded by Major-General John S Wood, and 6th Armoured under Major-General Robert W Grow. Grow's force, attacking south along the coast, was to exert the main effort, and on

Opposite page: The head of the Allied command structure: Montgomery, Eisenhower's deputy in overall command of all forces in France, talks with Bradley, Commander of First US Army, and Patton, Commander of Third US Army. The command was amended slightly for the exploitation phase. *Top:* A typical scene in Normandy. The animals provided occasional fresh food as well as cover. *Above:* If the hedgerow was tough for the tanks, open ground could be worse for infantry, giving the defenders clear fields of fire. *Right:* The hedge parapets provided some protection

Opposite page: Allied aircraft have worked well against French railroads.
This page: Coutances is added to the long list of towns wrecked in the fighting

the morning of 28th July he received the order to start. Combat Command A, in the van, reached Lessay, but were held up by mines, damaged bridges and congestion. After a short delay, the command passed through Lessay at last, and from then on enjoyed easy progress until they stopped for the night several miles to the south of Coutances. On their left flank Combat Command B of 4th Armoured Division set off on the morning of 28th July, and they too immediately ran into a minefield, which held up the advance for three hours. Following a similar pattern to Combat Command A, they finally cleared the minefield, and were able to make rapid and unhindered progress as far as Coutances. When they entered the city, a small group of defenders put up a brief but determined fight, but after that sharp exchange the city was in VIII Corps' hands.

At one time, Coutances had stood as the pinnacle of all the hopes of American achievement, but the situation had changed drastically. With the German Seventh Army on the run, Avranches was rapidly becoming the target: it was the gateway to Brittany: and, in view of the resistance being encountered in all other sectors, it was probably the only way out of Normandy, on to the Seine, and subsequently to Germany itself. On 29th July, with their sights therefore set firmly on Avranches, 6th and 4th Armoured Divisions again moved on south, with the more experienced 4th Armoured Division assigned the task of taking Avranches itself. General Wood, an inspired leader with the kind of flair and dash that Patton himself exhibited, ordered his Combat Command B to get to Avranches by any road to capture the town, and to secure the crossings to the east. Unknowingly, they passed within a few hundred yards of the German Seventh Army advanced command post to the north of Avranches, and just missed capturing Hausser. As he and his staff officers scuttled off across country in commandeered vehicles, the Americans entered Avranches, and enjoyed a pleasant surprise. This town was the vital point in the area from the point of view of both attack and defence. It contained the only road south within

Anti-tankgun

After the breakout, the advance to Avranches

ten miles of the coast; it was bounded on three sides by water; and it rose to a height of 200 feet where artillery could have commanding fields of fire overlooking the bridges across the See and Sélune rivers. Yet Avranches seemed virtually undefended. However, the capture of Avranches itself was not the ultimate achievement. For the Americans to be able to move on into Brittany unmolested, the bridges over the Sélune at Pontaubault had to be secure, and Middleton ordered Wood to pass on through the town and take them.

Before they could do so, trouble developed in Avranches. Columns of German soldiers, some in trucks marked with red crosses, appeared on the coastal road from Granville. The Americans let this column, ostensibly transporting wounded soldiers, pass on into Avranches, only to receive a blistering outburst of rifle fire from the trucks. When the Americans replied, the Germans promptly surrendered, and the trucks were found to contain ammunition and supplies. Several more Germans entered Avranches on 31st July, and another bout of fighting broke out, before they gave up the effort and several hundred surrendered into captivity, glad no doubt to be out of what they considered to be a lost war. From then on, the town was secure, and on the afternoon of 31st July Combat Command A of 4th Armoured Division raced on for the bridge at Pontaubault. They fought off a detachment of German reinforcements trying to beat them to it, and the Americans stood poised at the gates of Brittany. Kluge, at his Seventh Army Command Post in Le Mans, was in despair. 'The whole western front has been ripped open ...' he raged, 'the left flank has collapsed ...' And later: 'It's a madhouse here.'

Even as the Americans were making such fast and encouraging progress along the west coast of the peninsula, they were progressively rendering their flank more vulnerable, as Hitler was shortly to demonstrate. The further the American advances extended, the easier it was to cut off the spearhead by means of a westward attack against its flank. As VIII Corps moved along the coast towards Coutances, with the prospect of an advance as far as Avranches, the Allies needed a rapid push southwards in the centre of their lines, to prevent the Germans moving reinforcements towards the coast, to maintain the pressure on the disorganised enemy, and to provide the Allies themselves with a firm point on which they could pivot and come into line facing east for the next stage of the advance.

The key town in securing that pivot was Vire.

On the left of the VII Corps, XIX Corps, commanded by Major-General Charles H Corlett, was concerned in an attack towards Vire from the north-west. It was hoped that the advance would be only lightly opposed, as intelligence estimates promised resistance from only 3,000 Germans, supported by only scant artillery. However, it was on this front that Kluge had, since 27th July, been busy blocking the gap which was forming ominously between his LXXXIV Corps and II Parachute Corps, a gap which corresponded fairly closely with the boundary lines of the American XIX Corps. Into this gap Kluge plunged 2nd Panzer Division. By 28th July it was becoming obvious that the LXXXIV Corps front was breaking up, and Kluge needed more reinforcements west of the Vire. The 116th Panzer Division, recently arrived from the Pas de Calais, was taken out of Panzer Group West reserve into the front line, and ordered, with 2nd Panzer Division, to close the gap between Notre-Dames de-Cenilly and the Vire. Thus Corlett's XIX Corps, far from being unopposed, faced the freshest and strongest opposition on the entire front. It was 2nd Panzer Division which the Americans encountered first, at Tessy-sur-Vire.

Just north of Tessy, on the afternoon of 28th July, 30th Division under General Hobbs started down an open slope towards Troisgots. The 2nd Panzer Division, together with the remnants of 352nd Division, were waiting for them, in perfect defensive positions on a ridge just behind the stream running between Moyen and Troisgots. The Germans opened up with the most devastating fire from rifles, machine-guns, self-propelled guns, artillery, and tanks. It was an impassable blockage. General Hobbs tried

As the Americans fight each bound forwards . . .

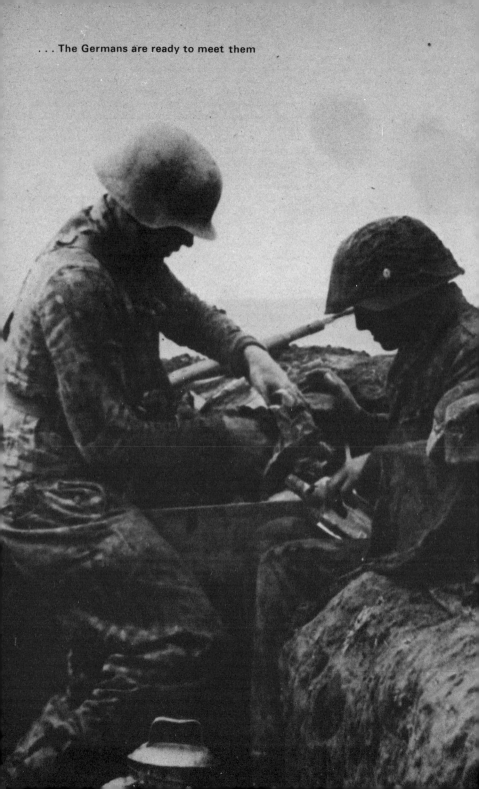

. . . The Germans are ready to meet them

again to move his troops forward on 29th July but once more they were stopped. On 30th July, after trying several other ways round the obstacle, Combat Command A skirted Ville-baudon to the south and turned to take Tessy from the west, but they also, after a tank battle lasting throughout that day, became tied down. Indeed 2nd Panzer Division mounted a counterattack which threatened to deprive the Americans of their position at Villebaudon and it was largely through the help of fighter bombers striking at Tessy that they were able to regain control. All through 30th and 31st July XIX Corps was held down firmly by German artillery fire, and made only limited advances.

On 1st August Corlett planned yet another attack against Tessy. Three tanks managed to get into the town before being repulsed, then troops of 120th Infantry reached the outskirts before they too were promptly ejected by the defenders. Finally, that afternoon, 22nd Infantry reached the centre of the town and got a firm hold on the crossings over the Vire, but even then they were subjected to constant shelling from nearby high ground. In all, Corlett's operation to take Vire had fallen short by some ten miles, but at least it had served to prevent 2nd Panzer Division, a force without doubt to be reckoned with, from moving further to the west to operate against the Americans in the coastal sector.

On the left of XIX Corps, V Corps were planning to move south in accordance with the progress made by the British on their own left flank. Aiming to reach the Souloeuvre/Vire river line, General Leonard T Gerow, the commander, faced the problem not only of his potentially exposed flank, but of a return to countryside similar to the hedgerow country of the previous weeks. The Germans took good advantage of the cover.

From the hills and hedges the Germans harassed V Corps with small-arms fire, mortar shelling, and artillery, and morale among the Americans plummetted. The commander of 9th Infantry found the going so hard that he asked to be replaced. His division commander, General Robertson, injected the right sort of spirit

back into the assault with the order 'Never mind these little pockets of resistance . . . Let's get down and take a bath in Vire.'

But enthusiasm itself was not enough. Kluge had pulled back II Parachute Corps into a strong defensive line around Torigny, and the Americans suffered 1,000 casualties. Then, as they were about to start a new offensive to clear the blockage, the Americans found that II Parachute Corps had withdrawn, and the grateful troops were able to advance unopposed. This phase of their advance came to an end not through any strong opposition from the Germans, but as a result of the simultaneous progress by the British on their left. At one stage the British advanced across the Americans' front and captured two bridges in their sector, with permission, it should be stated, though from whom it is not clear. Then British and American troops became intermingled and confused, and an immediate exploitation was out of the question. Finally, as 5th Division reached the Souloeuvre river on 1st August, the boundary lines were redrawn giving the British part of V Corp's sector.

This narrowing-down of V Corp's front was the direct result of British activity on their left flank. Montgomery had been endeavouring to assist the American advance by constant unremitting pressure in the eastern sector. Since the Canadians had failed to take the Bourguébus Ridge on the second day of Operation Cobra, and since the prospects of mounting another attack towards the Falaise plain were comparatively remote, Montgomery ordered Dempsey to carry out an attack in the Caumont area, using both British VIII and XXX Corps, and all his armour, to take the western half of the Mont Pinçon ridge and prevent the Germans using that high ground as an alternative pivot to Vire for their withdrawal. If, in their advance, the British were successful in getting behind the Germans as they tried to re-establish their defence facing westwards against the Americans, the effect could be devastating and the entire defensive structure facing the Allies would almost certainly disintegrate. This offensive was given the code name 'Operation Bluecoat'. The prospects for the attack were by no means favourable. Although the Germans had no armour in the area, and only one infantry division, they had been in possession of the ground for several weeks, and had dug themselves in firmly and laid minefields which would hinder progress. Moreover, they were assisted by the countryside, a region of *bocage* terrain among the most formidable in Normandy.

Dempsey's forces for the operation had been assembled with considerable speed and masterly organisation, in view of the limited period for planning and the difficulties of moving forces on the meagre road system. He had available, under his VIII Corps, the 11th Armoured Division, the Guards Armoured Division, 15th (Infantry) Division, and 6th Guards Tank Brigade. Under XXX Corps there were the 7th Armoured Division, the 43rd and 50th (Infantry) Divisions, and the 8th Armoured Brigade. The armoured strength altogether amounted to over 1,000 tanks.

The attack, like Goodwood and Cobra, was preceded by an intense air bombardment of the kind which, having proved so successful in those earlier operations, was now becoming an established pattern. It was extremely successful, and led to severe disorganisation in the German 365th

The Irish Guards on the eastern flank

Division, despite the low cloud which hampered visibility and caused 200 of the 1,300 bombers to return with their bomb loads intact. However, when the ground attacks began troubles immediately arose. On the left flank 43rd Division of XXX Corps ran into a minefield, and having cleared that it was stopped by a stream with banks too steep for the tanks, and which was in any case covered by several fire points which had survived the bombing. On the right flank the VIII Corps was more successful. The 11th Armoured Division, attacking on the right of the Corps front, set out with a new and largely experimental formation of two armoured and two infantry units operating as brigade groups. Traffic congestion, bad roads, pockets of resistance, and mines all conspired to slow down the advance, and by nightfall 11th Armoured had progressed no more than four miles. The 15th Division, however, fared far better. The 4th Tank Battalion of the Coldstream Guards pushed on without infantry support and by nightfall had gained Hill 309, with commanding views over all the countryside to the south.

That night, 30th/31st July, 11th Armoured Division laid the foundations for an attack during the following day in which it took over the lead once more. During darkness, an armoured car troop of 2nd Household Cavalry had patrolled beyond St Martin des Besaces and found a track through the

Another town liberated

Above: Burned-out vehicles litter the roads and fields round Caen. *Left:* Lieutenant-General B G Horrocks, who injected new life into XXX Corps' attack on Mont Pincon

Forêt l'Eveque which appeared to be unmined and undefended. In fact the forest stood astride the boundary between Seventh Army and Panzer Group West, and each appears to have thought that the other was taking care of its defence. The armoured cars travelled for five miles without opposition, and seized an unguarded bridge over the River Souloeuvre, west of le Bény Bocage. They called for support, and six tanks of the 2nd Northamptonshire Yeomanry arrived. All through that day this handful held on to the river crossing while the infantry set about clearing St Martin de Besaces, before they could push on that evening to reinforce these latter-day Horatios. The seizure of the bridge was an opportunity well taken. Though they had an exceptionally slender and vulnerable wedge into enemy territory, it was enough to enable 3rd RTR to cross to south of the river, turn eastwards, pass through le Bény Bocage, and seize a second bridge over the Souloeuvre from the south, behind the 21st Panzer Division. Thus they secured a valuable crossing point in the path of the Guards Division advance.

The move threw Kluge into great consternation. On the afternoon of 1st August British patrols were reconnoitring towards Vire, and that afternoon came within five miles of its northern outskirts. The projected hub of the German defence was thus in danger of falling. Kluge's only available reserve, 21st Panzer Division, was already in the line, and 9th SS Panzer Division, moving west from the Caen area, was unlikely to come into position for another 24 hours.

However, a happy accident served temporarily to extricate the Germans from a serious situation. Because of the progress of XIX Corps and V Corps of the US First Army, Dempsey ordered General Sir Richard O'Connor, commander of VIII Corps, to turn away from Vire, which stood in the path of Bradley's troops, and make instead for Flers to the south-east. This plan, though it seemed correct at the time, not only gave the Germans time to reorganise and strengthen the defences of Vire. It also led the British 11th Division into a head-on clash with the 9th SS Panzer Division, arriving from the Caen sector, who

mounted one of the best organised and most effective defences, in relation to their resources, of the campaign. They formed battle groups of two or three tanks, an infantry company, and a troop of *nebelwerfer* (six-barrelled rocket mortars). These small units infiltrated between the elongated British columns and harried the flanks.

The German troops were not numerous, and suffered from inadequate support and uncertain supply lines. Had 11th Division counterattacked at once the defence might well have collapsed, but they failed to seize the opportunity, and on 3rd August the attack came to a halt through the usual problem of having one unit advancing out of co-ordination with one of those on its flank. In this instance XXX Corps was at fault, as none of its three divisions was achieving its objectives on schedule. Dempsey tried to remedy the situation by firing the corps commander, Lieutenant-General G C Bucknall, and the commander of 7th Armoured Division, Major-General G W E J Erskine. The new corps commander, the forceful Lieutenant-General B G (later Sir Brian) Horrocks, fired XXX Corps with some enthusiasm, and it immediately redeemed its reputation with a notable feat of arms. On the night of 5th August, two tank troops of 13/18th Hussars, after unsuccessfully attacking the vital Mont Pinçon ridge the previous day, found an unguarded track up its west side, and all but one tank, which overturned on the steep and winding route, managed to reach the summit. That night infantrymen of the 4th Wilts stormed the slopes and Mont Pinçon was safe.

Even so, this important acquisition failed to aid the Allies as much as was expected. The Germans still held on tenaciously in the area, checking further advances, and even the fall of Vire to the Americans failed to dislodge the German defence on the eastern flank. However, by this time, important and spectacular developments at the other end of the line were taking the limelight, as Patton continued the exploitation along the coast, and threatened to break out of Normandy and into Brittany.

Third Army rampage

The selection of Normandy for the invasion was based to a large extent on the capacity of the Normandy and Brittany peninsulas to accommodate large quantities of incoming supplies. Even if the early days of the invasion required the provision of artificial harbours, the coastline of this part of north west France, within 500 miles, contained the ports of Rouen and Le Havre, Cherbourg, St Malo, Brest, Lorient, Vannes, St Nazaire, and Nantes, as well as innumerable smaller harbours. If these, or even some of them, could be captured intact, or restored to working order within a short time, they would provide the capacity for the massive build-up of supplies, weapons, and ammunition required for the advanced stages of the invasion.

On 10th July General Eisenhower set down in a letter to Montgomery the importance of capturing the Brittany peninsula: 'The ideal situation would be to obtain the entire coastal area from Havre to Nantes, both inclusive. With such a broad avenue of entry we could bring into Europe every single soldier the United States could procure for us, and we would have . . . little interest in Anvil (the invasion in Southern France scheduled for 15th August).'

For the Brittany operation, General Patton's US Third Army was to come into being. As already noted. Bradley had informally given Patton control of the VIII Corps in the advance towards Avranches, and at noon on 1st August, with the approval of Montgomery and Eisenhower, the 12th Army Group became operational under Bradley himself, with Patton taking over the Third Army and Hodges the First Army.

Bradley's orders to Patton were to move south, and first secure St Hilaire, Fougères, and Rennes, to give ample room for manoeuvre, even for withdrawal should it be necessary. Then he was to turn westwards and take St Malo, Brest, and the Quiberon Bay area, where it was planned to build an entirely new port complex to make up for the loss of port installations destroyed by the retreating Germans. Finally he could turn his attention to

Help for a beaten enemy

the rest of Brittany. Patton's interpretation of these orders was liberal, to say the least. He planned to drive south west straight through Rennes to the Quiberon Bay area, to cut off the Germans in the peninsula from reinforcements, and to sever their escape route. He then planned to clear the entire plateau of the peninsula, forcing the Germans into a few pockets in the ports along the coast. Then he would turn round for his ultimate mission, the drive eastwards to the Seine and Paris. Bradley's concern for a wide corridor to ensure the safety of the column was thrown high into the wind.

Patton was a cavalryman. His method was to slice dramatically across the country to distant objectives, and he reckoned that in Brittany he could leave the flanks to look after themselves. The campaign that was to follow was typical of his character and training, and he was fortunate in taking command of units led by men such as Wood and Grow who understood and sympathised with his methods, and worked and thought as he did.

Patton himself was one of the most flamboyant and colourful of all the war's generals, eccentric though so many of them were. How much his manner was purposely affected, to be in keeping with the 'wild west' tradition, and how much of it was genuine, is hard to say. Certainly, even though he appeared the tough and hard commander, he was in fact extremely sensitive, and, like Churchill, capable of being moved to tears. Patton had placed his career in jeopardy in Sicily during 1943, when he slapped two young soldiers suffering respectively from dysentry and shellshock, which in each case he took to be cowardice; but he had survived without a major public scandal and had retained his high position. Possibly his only real fault, in a general whose principal and most useful characteristic was exuberance, was a tendency to allow that very quality to carry him away. What Patton constantly needed was a superior of calmer judgement, a Montgomery or a Bradley, to temper his enthusiasms and keep the correct targets in view.

In his military thinking, Patton was the quintessential cavalryman: bold, dashing, forceful, aggressive. In his book *War as I Knew It*, he states that he favoured 'a good plan violently executed now' rather than a 'perfect plan next week'. And to achieve these plans, he set his subordinate generals far-reaching objectives, then left them free to get on with working out the details themselves, believing that you should 'never tell people how to do things. Tell them what to do, and they will surprise you with their ingenuity.'

Patton's mode of operation became apparent soon after he took over command of Third Army. Far from carefully fulfilling Bradley's requirement for a wide corridor into Brittany, Patton confidently sent his divisions racing through the narrowest of gaps, the single bridge at Avranches. Despite one of the few serious air attacks of the whole campaign by the Luftwaffe, in which they used the entire bombing capacity of Luftflotte III, the move was a spectacular success. Patton stationed senior officers at Avranches and Pontaubault and, at the entrance to the bottleneck, they herded traffic on down the road in any order. As the tanks, trucks, and guns reached the point where the roads radiated off west and south into Brittany, other senior officers channelled them out into their appropriate route. While AA guns held off the attacking bombers, Patton was able to move seven divisions down that single road in seventy-two hours. One officer remarked: 'Still spending most of my time as a traffic cop.' It was not the textbook method, but it was certainly effective.

The first of the units to move out into Brittany was Combat Command A of General Wood's 4th Armoured Division, which sped southwards and reached the outskirts of Rennes, the important road and communications centre at the base of the peninsula. There they were stopped by 88mm anti-aircraft guns manned by men of the Luftwaffe, supported by small arms and anti-tank guns. While reinforcements raced to the city to consolidate the defence, the Germans not only survived an attack by American Thunderbolt fighters and artillery, but also managed to knock out eleven American tanks. General Wood was soon given reason to ponder the wis-

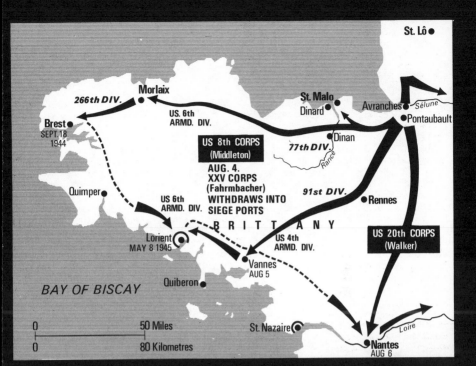

Into the heart of Brittany

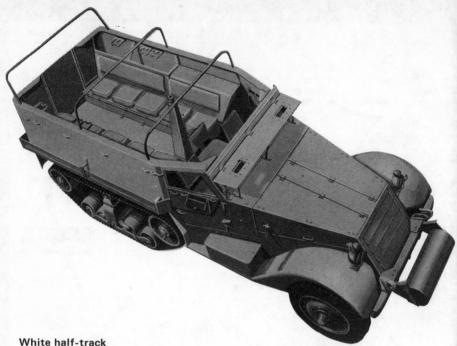

White half-track
Crew/payload: Thirteen men. *Combat weight:* 17,650 pounds.
Length: 21 feet 7 inches. *Maximum speed:* 45 mph. *Maximum range:* 220 miles.
Armament: One .3 inch machine gun. *Engine:* 148 hp

M10
Crew: Five men. *Combat weight:* 63,000 pounds. *Width:* 10 feet.
Length: 19 feet 6½ inches. *Maximum speed:* 28 mph. *Maximum range:* 160 miles.
Armament: One .3 inch (76.2mm) gun, one .5 inch machine gun and one
.3 inch machine gun. *Engine:* 500 hp Ford

dom of all-out advance. His division was stretched to the limits along a fifty-five mile line. Communications and supplies were in severe jeopardy, and mortar and artillery fire rained down on Combat Command A. Wood sent off urgent messages calling for immediate supplies, for an additional infantry combat team and for air cover, including fighter-bomber support from dawn to dusk. The next day, in response to his request, Middleton, the VIII Corps commander, let Wood know that the 13th Infantry regiment was on the way to Rennes to lend support, and until that unit and the remainder of 4th Armoured Division arrived, Wood kept up a series of counterattacks to keep the Germans occupied.

It was at this stage that Wood came up with a plan which was to mark him as one of the most far-sighted of the American commanders, and which would set him for a time at odds with his more conservative thinking superiors. Wood was already sensing that the campaign in Brittany was slowly being relegated to only secondary importance in the post-invasion period. If 4th Armoured Division itself could reach Rennes in such a short swift stroke, and then go on to the coast in the Quiberon Bay area, Brittany would be cut off from the rest of France. Why, then, engage valuable armoured divisions in a long and possibly costly campaign to clear the whole peninsula of comparatively few German troops, only to have them stand on the shores of the Atlantic with little more to do than paddle in the sea while the battle raged at an increasing distance to the east of them? Wood could already see that the important ports were not in Brittany, but in northern France and Belgium, that the main battles were going to be fought not in the peninsula, but far to the east. And he wanted to be in at the kill.

Wood's plan was for his 4th Armoured Division to leave the reduction of the resistances at Rennes to the 8th Infantry Division when it arrived, while his armour bypassed the city in a wide circle to the west, and came into line facing eastwards between Rennes and Nantes. The manoeuvre would block German communications into

and out of the peninsula, and leave the armour in an excellent position to attack eastwards towards Chateaubriant and Angers.

Moreover, if the 4th Armoured Division then attacked towards Angers, it would achieve the isolation of the peninsula quite as effectively as if it took the Quiberon Bay area, and would be infinitely better placed for the move east. Feeling perfectly confident that his plan would be approved without hesitation, Wood recommended to corps headquarters that he should be allowed to push on to Angers, and at the same time ordered the plan to be carried out.

No doubt he was disappointed when orders arrived re-affirming Quiberon Bay as his target. That order had in fact been sent before receipt of Wood's new idea, and Wood had no alternative but to comply, while he went on trying to get his plan approved. During the next four days, however, Wood could get no clear go-ahead. Firstly he was instructed to 'secure Rennes' before he continued. Then he was given a new task, to block the enemy retreat from Rennes. This he failed to do, and before the 4th Armoured Division entered the town on August 4th some 2,000 Germans had destroyed military installations in the city and were moving in groups across country to St Nazaire, which they reached five days later. With Rennes captured, Middleton permitted a compromise, not allowing Wood to go east, nor forcing him to go west, but instructing him to take the bridges over the River Vilaine south of Rennes. Wood, however, failed to receive this order, and radioed for a mission. At this stage Middleton felt the time had come for a visit to 4th Armoured Division headquarters, where Wood was delighted to see him, and threw his arms around the corps commander in welcome. He had chance, at last, to air his grievances, and complained: 'They are winning the war the wrong way.' Wood won Middleton partly over to his views, and again they agreed on a compromise. Wood secured permission to remain facing eastwards, while agreeing to send a small force westwards to secure the Vilaine river. Finally the situation was abruptly resolved. The army chief of staff, General Gaffey,

Right: Major-General John S Wood, 4th Armored Division commander, and one of the most able generals in Brittany. *Below:* American armoured vehicles dominate the scene. The people of Fougères (bottom) appear to have been expecting them. *Opposite page:* American half tracks, tanks and infantrymen spread out into Brittany

U.S.A. 6035718 S

CAFE F SALMON

saw the arrangement, and ordered 4th Armoured Division to comply with Patton's orders and move on westwards towards Vannes and Lorient.

On 5th August Wood sent off his Combat Command A to Vannes. They moved with commendable speed, raced the seventy miles to the town in seven hours, and snatched control of its key points from the surprised Germans.

On the following day, Wood sent off an optimistic message to General Patton: 'Have Vannes, will have Lorient this evening.' And he also raised again the question of a move out of Brittany: 'Trust we can turn around and get headed in the right direction soon.'

They did not take Lorient that night, and on 7th August Wood recommended to Middleton that the infantry should take over the task of capturing Lorient, and said: 'We should be allowed to reassemble and get ready to hit again in a more profitable direction, namely to Paris.' When he was ordered to carry on and take his present objectives, and even having done so to wait in the vicinity, Wood's appeals became almost plaintive: 'Am being left pretty far out on this limb.' It was not until 15th August that he finally secured permission to drive eastwards, and handed over the task of containing Lorient to 6th Armoured Division.

Ten years after the event, Wood was to state that he believed the decision to move his armoured division away from the pursuit of the disorganised enemy and towards Lorient was one of the great mistakes of the war. And two years later still, in 1956, Middleton gave his judgement. He told the American army's military historians: 'Wood was right, of course,' though he added, pinpointing the difficulties which so often arise when events run ahead of plans: 'But the High Command at the time was absolutely right in wanting the ports.'

While Wood, in the field, was hammering away to turn his armour in the right direction, at headquarters military thinking was gradually, but rather more slowly, coming to the same conclusions, as SHAEF planners turned attention away from the Brittany operation towards the more fruitful task of destroying the Seventh

Army in Normandy, while leaving only one corps to capture Brittany. On August 2nd Eisenhower forecast that in the next two or three days Bradley would open the enemy's western flank, and that the Allies would then be free to select the next move at will. Then, he thought, it would no longer be necessary to deploy large forces for the conquest of Brittany, and he would be able to devote the major part of his forces to the destruction of the German armies west of the Orne river.

The next day, 3rd August, Bradley put this notion in more tangible form, and told Patton that he was to clear Brittany with a minimum of forces, as the main mission for the Americans was to drive eastward and expand the continental lodgement area.

Brittany was thus relegated to the status of a secondary campaign, while Montgomery on 9th August summed up the new thinking: 'The main business lies to the east.' It was primarily an indication of the enormous success of Cobra, and a clear sign that the post invasion period was at least going in the required direction.

As the 4th Armoured Division prepared to move east, the operation in the Brittany peninsula was thus left in the hands of 6th Armoured Division. Commanded by General Robert W. Grow, this division, which had moved into Brittany directly on the heels of 4th Armoured, set to work with the same dash and enthusiasm as its predecessors.

On 1st August Grow was ordered to move his division down the road through Pontaubault, and on to Dinan, less than forty miles away. It was not an inspiring mission to set the corps, but Grow got on with the job, and his plans for its execution were approved by Middleton. Then, later that day, Patton himself turned up and put a new complexion on the entire picture. He had, he announced, laid a five pound bet with Montgomery that his troops would be in Brest 'by Saturday night'. Grow's division was the one to carry out the assignment, and Patton gave Grow his order with elegant and dramatic simplicity: 'Take Brest.' Intermediate objectives were to be ignored, except for the railway from Brest to Rennes, and the division was to bypass resistance. This new mission, 200 miles away with little to worry about until they got there, was enough to satisfy even Grow, but it was to lead to problems between Middleton and Grow similar to those which had arisen between Middleton and Wood. At a conference late on 2nd August, Grow's fellow officers still had no inkling that Patton had issued this new order, which was still only verbal to the corps commander. One of them counselled firmly against advancing too quickly across the peninsula, and called attention to the need for supply bases, and for the division itself to move in a compact formation, without becoming strung out dangerously across the length of the peninsula.

Only after hearing this advice, it appears, did Grow let on that he had been given the task of taking Brest, and his statement was received with gasps of astonishment.

Grow's new mission had remained unannounced up the line, it seems, as well as down. The division began its advance at noon on the 4th August, and after Pontaubault was split into two columns, based on Combat Commands A and B. The former ran into a fight at Mauron, having missed its turn at a crossroads, and the latter covered more than thirty miles before receiving the order to halt. Such an early interruption, with the objective still in the far distance, and progress as yet going reasonably well, threw the division into consternation. Later it was expanded, as a message arrived from Middleton instructing Grow to protect his front and concentrate so that he could move in on St Malo and Dinan on the following day. Grow made a gesture towards compliance by moving his columns into the appropriate formation, while at the same time he sent off an officer with a request to corps headquarters that the mission should be changed. The answer was a terse and abrupt refusal.

On the morning of 4th August General Patton again arrived to see Grow, unannounced, and seemed outraged at finding Grow's divisional staff sitting in a cornfield making plans for the action against Dinan, instead of racing across Brittany towards Brest. He demanded to know why they were stationary, and Grow explained that they were complying with a corps order. He even had on the spot the note he had received from Middleton. Patton read the note, was thoughtful for a moment, then made a muttered comment about Middleton. He said that he would 'see Middleton', and ordered the division to go right ahead where he had told them to go.

It had been a confusing situation, but now that Patton personally had clarified it, Grow's division set off once more at high speed to take Brest. They were too late. There was no making up the time lost, and when the first of his troops, Combat Command B, reached the outskirts of Brest on the morning of 7th August they ran into stiff resistance from the garrison which had withdrawn into the town. Grow tried to bluff the Germans into surrender. In a jeep draped in white and carrying a flag of truce, he sent an officer and a sergeant who spoke German into the garrison to offer peace terms to the Germans. When they reached German lines, the Americans were blindfolded and conducted to an underground command post, where they confronted a group of officers. The sergeant handed over Grow's offer of a surrender, which was promptly handed back to him, and he then proceeded to read it aloud in German. The senior German present, Mosel, confirmed that he understood the message, but declined to surrender. Salutes were exchanged, and the two Americans were taken back to the German front line, and released in their jeep.

There was no choice but to attack. As it happened, the attack failed, and it was not until mid-Spetember that three infantry divisions, after a ten day operation, finally took control of Brest. Nevertheless, Grow's operation in reaching Brest so quickly and clearing most of the interior of the peninsula was carried out with great skill and panache. Grow, perhaps with some justification, later described it as the greatest cavalry-type operation of the war. He, like Wood and like their superior Patton, had proved himself a bold and farseeing commander who revelled in being given assignments deep into enemy territory. And he, like Wood, had been frustrated by the dictates of caution on the part of one

A patrol moves along the front of the Casino at Dinard

Riflemen in action.

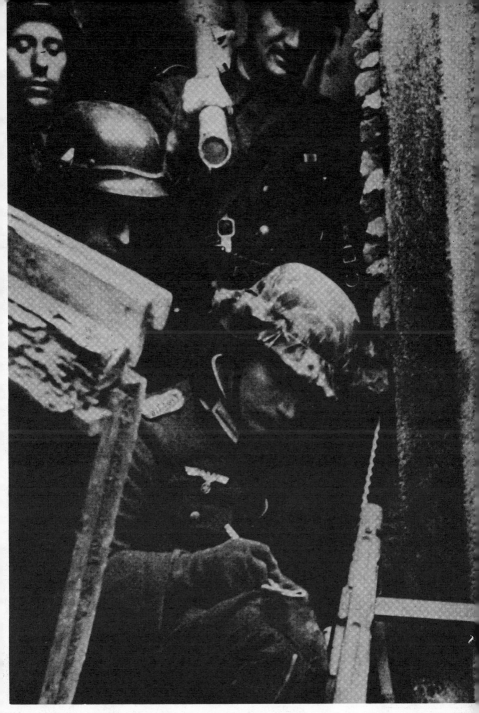

Opposite page: Pipe-smoking *panzerfaust* grenadier digs himself a foxhole. *Above:* Young officer briefs his unit

American tanks roll forward unopposed

of his superiors. The one question which remains open is whether, had he not been diverted to Dinan, he could have reached Brest one day earlier, taken the Germans completely off their guard, and captured the city. It is a question which can never now be raised above the blurred realms of speculation. It should be recalled, however, in fairness to Middleton, that he was constantly dealing with the problems of an entire corps and was constantly expected to see the role of that corps in relation to the circumstances of the Third Army, even of the entire invading force. Had the fortunes of the 6th and 4th Armoured Divisions gone wildly wrong, Middleton would no doubt have gone down in history as an irresponsible commander who recklessly sacrificed his divisions or ignored true objectives. For while gambling always afterwards looks brilliant if it is successful, the gambler is generally blamed if he fails. There is every place in the conduct of a war for the counsel of caution.

Grow's and Wood's brilliant exploits apart, at this stage in the campaign yet another corps was contributing to the reputation of Patton's army, and simultaneously of course to the successful fighting of the war. This was XV Corps, under Major-General Wade H Haislip. General Haislip had set up headquarters in France in the middle of July, with a view to taking part in the campaign to secure Brittany, but the success of Operating Cobra, and the new strategic thinking, appeared to make the use of three corps in that peninsula unnecessary.

On 1st August Haislip received his first information to this effect, when he was told that the projected operation of his corps to the south west had been cancelled, and that a new operation would be started towards the south east. To achieve this XV Corps was to move in between VII Corps and VIII Corps, to widen the corridor at Avranches, relieve the congestion, and render the exit from Normandy to Brittany more secure. The 90th Division, which had left the Normandy *bocage* country with a tarnished reputation through lack of aggression, was given a new commander, Brigadier-General Raymond S McLain, and assigned the task of capturing St Hilaire-du-Harcouet, and setting up a defensive position there to stop the movement of German troops westwards between the See and Sélune rivers. The 90th Division promptly and efficiently set about refurbishing its reputation, and two

task forces, racing across open ground in the face of enemy artillery fire, took the bridge and town, and set up a secure defensive line from St Hilaire to Juvigny. On 2nd August, 79th Division moved in on their right, and the corps was left facing south east for the next move. It was then that Patton told Haislip, informally, that he should not be surprised if he received orders to move to the north-east or even to the north. It was the first real indication of the course of events which was to lead to the climax of the Normandy battle.

In the meantime, Haislip assigned the next objectives to 79th and 90th Divisions: Laval and Mayenne respectively. The opposing forces were ill-organised and thin on the ground, and by the night of 5th August both towns were in XV Corps hands. Gradually, the line of advance for the Corps was turned, anti-clockwise, towards the rear of the German forces defending against the Normandy invaders, as the next project was set at Le Mans, some forty-five miles due east of Laval. Haislip showed that he was cast in the same mould as Wood and Grow when he told his commanders to push all personnel to the limit of human endurance. They did, and by 9th August both 79th and 90th Divisions had entered Le Mans.

Thus not only did 90th Division restore its confidence and prove itself the equal of any other division then in the fighting (an improvement which won for McLain the Bronze Oak Leaf Cluster to his DSC) but XV Corps, with a fast and aggressive move, showed how well it could carry out the kind of action Patton wanted for his army.

Now the broad pattern of the campaign was emerging. On the eastern flank, the Allies were making slow and expensive progress. On the western flank, their right, they were circling around the enemy like the jaws of some gigantic trap. Patton had already remarked to Haislip that a turn to the north was a possibility to be born in mind, and if that were to take place, the jaws of the trap might well snap shut. It was apparent that Hitler, if he was to rescue his Seventh Army, would have to order an immediate withdrawal to the east. But Hitler, ever unpredictable, did no such thing. Instead of saving his army, he seemed intent on pushing its head even deeper into the trap. Perhaps his decision was not meant as a sacrificial gesture. It certainly turned out to be a suicidal one.

Hitler hits back

On 2nd August, determined not to accept the need for an immediate withdrawal to the Seine, Hitler ordered Kluge to stabilise the front in Normandy by means of a strong armoured counterattack to Avranches. Hitler promised extensive reinforcements for the attack, but this promise did little to solve Kluge's problem – how to amass sufficient forces to carry out the attack with any prospect of success. It was obvious from the beginning that his resources were slim, but in view of the tactical situation, Kluge was reluctant to postpone the attack even for twenty-four hours: he faced heavy pressure on the north in the region of the See river, and in the south he was being constantly threatened by the enveloping movements of the US Third Army. Worst of all, it was evident that if the Allies discovered any build-up of German forces for the attack, they would, with their undisputed air superiority, turn out in force with fighters and bombers and blast the assembling forces before the attack got off the ground.

The very intentions of the counter-attack were in dispute. Kluge planned only to reach Avranches and regain the defensive line in Normandy, in order to cover a withdrawal to a new defensive line behind the Seine. Hitler wanted to mount a massive attack with all the forces that could be assembled, to take Avranches, then turn to the north east against the US First Army flank, cutting off the Third Army and neutralising the American breakout. But Hitler was not at the front. He was trying to plan the defence of France from his headquarters at Berchtesgaden, and exactly how far out of touch with the situation he was is demonstrated by the fact that on 7th August, well after the attack had begun, he was still issuing orders outlining its broad aims: 'The decision in the battle of France depends on the success of the attack. The C-in-C West has a unique opportunity which will never return to drive into an extremely exposed enemy area and thereby to change the situation completely.'

Hitler at least, however, showed sufficient realism to agree to back up the attack with all the available reinforcements, including the reserve of the Luftwaffe, amounting to 1,000 fighters. In addition, an armoured division and six infantry divisions were on their way to reinforce the front, both from the south of France and from the Pas de Calais, where it was obvious by now that no other invasion could be expected. These forces should have brought the armoured strength for the operation up to eight divisions, although when it got under way only four had been assembled, with less than 190 tanks between them.

The attack was scheduled to begin at 2200 hours on 6th August, but was then postponed until shortly after midnight on the morning of 7th August. The plan provided for an attack by three armoured divisions moving abreast. On the right 116th Panzer Division was to advance along the north bank of the See River towards Cherence. In the centre the reinforced 2nd Panzer Division was to move along the south bank of the See, and 2nd SS Panzer Division, also reinforced, was to cover the left flank and attack on both sides of Mortain. Behind them a fourth armoured division, 1st SS Panzer Division, was to exploit the initial success, pass through the front line, and take Avranches.

The opening phase of the attack met with considerable success. The 2nd SS Panzer Division advanced swiftly to Mortain and took the town by storm, moving on then towards high ground around St Hilaire. It seemed that it might even reach Avranches, but they ran into trouble in the region of Hill 317, a knot of high ground east of Mortain, where the Americans held possession. With its commanding views in every direction, it had been among the first targets the Americans thought of taking when they moved into Mortain on 3rd August. Now 2nd SS Panzer Division's surprise attack had isolated a rifle battalion of 30th Division on that hill, and a few men fought stubbornly and heroically to retain possession of the commanding heights. For some time, too, they fought alone, for First Army headquarters failed to recognise the attack as more than a local effort. At dawn on 7th August the Americans

began to regain their senses and realise that if the Germans crossed the See river the entire exploitation of the breakout might be jeopardised. General Hobbs, 30th Division commander, also seemed to play down the effect of the attack and almost declined an offer from VII Corps of a regiment of 4th Division to reinforce his defence. It was only at noon that day that the corps headquarters came to the conclusion that the Germans had launched a major counterattack to separate the First and Third Armies.

And it was 30th Division which bore the brunt of the assault. More than ten German battalions of artillery, infantry, and tanks had got behind the American positions, where they severed communications, killed messengers, raided command posts, and inflicted 600 casualties on the division. To help out, 4th Division laid effective artillery fire on the enemy's flank, and in the clear August skies fighter bombers harassed the German tanks throughout the day, knocking out on 7th August alone some forty of the seventy which had penetrated the American lines.

In the centre of the attack 2nd Panzer Division moved off shortly after dawn on 7th August, and reached almost to Juvigny before it was stopped by anti-tank fire and artillery from American positions on both sides of the See river.

The 116th Panzer Division, scheduled to attack towards Cherences, failed to attack altogether, as a result of a curious *crise de confidence* on the part of its commander, General Gerhard Graf von Schwerin. As one of the participants in the plot on Hitler's life on 20th July, he seems to have had no heart for the counterattack, and refused to allow his division to play any part in it. At 1600 hrs that day Hausser sacked him. Thirty minutes later, under a new commander, Colonel Walter Reinhard, the division started its advance, and straight away became bogged down. As for the planes that were to support the ground forces, they were dealt with by Allied pilots as soon as they took off, and not a single aircraft reached the battle area.

The attack went no further, and on the afternoon of 7th August, Hitler

With ample determination but little hope of success, the Germans prepare to carry out the Mortain counterattack

Briefly, Hitler's divisions are back on the offensive

Opposite page: Every infantryman's
problem. *This page, top:* Pause behind
the front line. *Above:* A minor casualty.
Right: Rest period

Covering fire from machine gun post

concluded that Kluge had failed. He blamed Kluge for launching the offensive too soon, before three of the promised divisions had assembled, and for directing the main effort to the north of Mortain rather than towards St Hilaire. But he nevertheless pressed on with the idea of an attack to isolate Third Army, and while Kluge on the afternoon of 7th August was thinking of a hasty withdrawal, Hitler, deliberately or otherwise, appeared to remain in ignorance of the true state of affairs, and launched forth on an eloquent tirade of words which seemed now to be the principal weapon in the limited armoury he could bring to bear against the Americans: 'I command the attack be prosecuted daringly and recklessly to the sea, regardless of the risk. Greatest daring, determination, imagination must give wings to all echelons of command. Each and every man must believe in victory. Cleaning up in rear areas and in Brittany can wait until later.' And since Hitler was the supreme commander, and his order left positively no room for manoeuvre, Kluge had no choice but to obey.

In a sense Hitler was right, and Bradley afterwards admitted that an attack to the south of Mortain, where the American defences were thinner on the ground, might have been successful: 'Had the enemy side-slipped his Panzers several thousand yard south he might have broken through to Avranches that very first day.' But the enemy had not done so, and Bradley's promptitude in deploying 4th Armoured Division against the main weight of the attack, plus 30th Division's tenacity at Hill 317, plus a counterattack by 2nd Armoured on the 8th from the south towards Mortain, had served to frustrate the effort.

The Germans had spent most of the daylight hours on 7th August digging in to avoid the ferocious weight of the air and artillery bombardment, and Kluge that night was faced with the problem of finding some way to regain the impetus. In the event, it was not to be regained at all, for twenty-four hours after the Mortain counterattack went in, new and spectacular moves were beginning on the eastern flank of the Normandy front line.

There the II Canadian Corps launched a spectacular operation southwards along the Caen-Falaise road. That operation will be dealt with shortly, but to avoid the confusion of moving haphazardly from one area of the battlefield to the other, it will be convenient to stay with the Mortain sector for the time being, bearing in mind that the activity on the Canadian front was exerting a significant effort on the German outlook. When the Germans estimated that some 600 tanks had attacked south towards Falaise during the night of 7th/8th August, they were plunged into deep consternation, the more so because one armoured division, 10th SS Panzer Division, was already moving out of the Canadian sector to bolster the forces for the renewed attack which Hitler demanded towards Avranches. In the event, there was time to cancel the orders for two other armoured divisions to move, and retain them as part of the defences against the Canadians.

The new Mortain attack was at first scheduled for 9th August, but was delayed owing to developments north of Falaise, and in the end Hitler, anxious that this second attack should not fail like the first through being launched too early, reserved the designation of H-Hour for himself. He also, uncharacteristically, allowed withdrawals in other sectors, and ordered no attacks to take place which might cause casualties and drain his numerical strength. He was banking a great deal on the attack to Avranches. But in the end, even Hitler's blind unnerving will was denied, both by circumstances and by his own commanders. Eberbach, the Panzer Group West Commander, concluded that he could not attack until 20th August since only then would he have the necessary reinforcements, and only then would the waning moon provide the darkness needed for protection from Allied air and artillery. Furthermore, the American XV Corps was now carrying out the move to the north projected by Patton to Haislip, and this, together with the Canadian push from Caen towards Falaise, gave Kluge the first inkling that he was facing the prospect of being trapped. On 10th August Kluge mooted the idea at last of calling off the attack

General Heinrich Eberbach, Commander of Fifth Panzer Army, in charge of the counterattack

spelled the end of Hitler's projected attack towards the sea – and the end of any chance the German armies might have had of cutting off the American Third Army.

Was there ever any chance at all? There is no doubt that the attack caught the Americans off their guard in unprepared positions, and as Bradley admitted, an attack in the more southerly direction could well have taken Avranches. Even so, the overall effect might not have been so far-reaching as Hitler had hoped. Even had the Third Army positions south of Avranches become logistically untenable, a possibility which some officers had foreseen, and with the Brittany ports still not in a position to supply them, there was still the air. During the counterattack, aircraft were standing by to drop in 2,000 tons of supplies per day to the troops in Brittany, and with the Allies holding total air superiority, there was little danger of being completely isolated. And had the Germans reached Avranches, it is hard to see what they would have done with it. American tank and artillery support in the area was so strong that the Germans would have been hard pressed to achieve more than local gains, mainly by infiltration. In the end, it can only be concluded that the Americans, at least on the western flank, were now too mobile, too well equipped, and too confident to let the Germans force them back into the static warfare of the weeks in the Cotentin.

That the Americans were not now going to let go easily the superiority they had toiled so hard to win is illustrated by one sustained example of their determination, the battle for Hill 317. There, between 7th August and 12th August, the 2nd Battalion, 30th Infantry maintained its hold on a position which gave them a clear view of the battle around Mortain. Fortunately, when the battalion command post was overrun on 7th August, the men isolated on the hill included two observers of the 230th Field Artillery Battalion, who directed a steady stream of accurate artillery fire on to the Germans positions around the hill. As 2nd SS Panzer Grenadier Division tried to dislodge them, they kept up the fight, and

towards Avranches, and turning instead to the south-east to strike at the spearhead of the American salient pushing north. On 11th August Kluge discussed the situation with Hausser and Eberbach, and together these three concluded that the situation on the left (southern) flank of their armies in the west was so bad as to merit immediate measures, including the deployment there of armour, which would render impossible the projected attack to Avranches, and make it essential to withdraw from the Mortain area. As a result of these consultations, Kluge wrote to Hitler recommending that Seventh Army withdraw from Mortain and assemble its forces near Carrouges to attack on 14th August.

Hitler generally concurred, while reserving it as his ultimate intention to attack towards the sea in the west, and permitted a minor withdrawal of the forces at Mortain, prior to an attack at the flank of the American XV Corps. The withdrawal took place on the night of 11th August and it

Infantry patrol

even took several prisoners. Small artillery spotter planes tried to drop supplies to them, but were frustrated by anti-aircraft fire, although a cargo plane succeeded in dropping one day's supply of food and ammunition.

In more picturesque style – if such is possible in the conditions of war – the

230th Field Artillery Battalion loaded smoke-shell cases with medical supplies, and shot them over the heads of the surrounding Germans on to the hill. When that system proved success-ful, other artillery units joined in, and the bandages and morphine thus made available served admirably to treat the many wounded men on the hill and maintained morale. As for

food, the battalion was sustained largely by French civilian farmers, who kept it supplied with poultry and vegetables, and of course ran the risk of reprisal should the Germans eventually succeed in overrunning the defended territory. When they eventually were relieved by 35th Division, the troops on the hill had suffered 300 casualties, wounded and killed, but another 300 walked off the hill unharmed. Most significantly, at the height of their peril, the soldiers on the hill had reported that they were 'not too worried' about the situation so long as the artillery fire continued. That unshakeable confidence, more than anything else, was the measure of the superiority of the American forces in the western sector.

Canadian setbacks

Operation Totalize, the Canadian attack down the Caen/Falaise Road mentioned in the preceding chapter, was not specifically intended as the uppermost of the set of 'jaws' closing round the bulk of the German Seventh Army. When it was first visualised, there was no sign of any westward movement by the German Panzers, nor of their attack towards Avranches. Montgomery's intention was still to drive the Germans back against the Seine, and destroy them before they could make an organised crossing. They were already evidently off balance, and the need was for a continued pressure to keep them in that condition. It looked as if the Germans were trying to pivot their retreat on a 'hinge' just to the south of Caen, and the operation was designed to knock away that hinge. The task was given to Canadian First Army, which had now come into existence, and comprised Canadian II Corps and British I Corps, under the command of Lieutenant-General H D G Crerar, and operating in the sector east of the Orne river.

Directly on his front, Crerar faced

Lieutenant General Sir Henry D G Crerar, Commander of First Canadian Army

only one armoured and three infantry divisions, four other armoured divisions having been moved westwards across the Orne. Nevertheless, the Canadian task was not an easy one. The Germans were still holding excellent positions, and they were well equipped with 88mm dual purpose guns, but this did not prevent the Canadians from being relatively optimistic. General Crerar's basic philosophy for attack depended on the achievement of maximum surprise, which he considered as important as maximum fire-power. Crerar had elucidated his idea earlier that summer in the following terms:

'In the 'break-in' attack against an organized enemy position, a matter of highest importance is to get the infantry over and through the enemy's prearranged zones of defensive fire in the shortest possible time after the intention to attack has been revealed . . . It is essential that the fire and movement should be positively and very closely integrated at the outset.

The attack itself was entrusted to Canadian II Corps, commanded by Lieutenant-General G G Simonds, a young (he was only forty-one when he took command of the corps in the preceding January), forceful and original soldier. On 1st August he explained that the essence of the problem was how to get armour through the enemy gun screen to sufficient depth to disrupt the anti-tank gun and mortar defence, when the country was suited to their combined use. Simonds foresaw that this could be done by means of overwhelming air support to destroy or neutralise enemy tanks, anti-tank guns, and mortars, and by infiltrating through the screen in bad visibility to a sufficient depth to destroy the second line of defence. He proposed to dispense with an artillery bombardment, in order to avoid disclosing his intentions, and to attack at night to deprive the enemy fire of its accuracy. After the first phase of the attack, the second phase was to begin the following day and in this the infantry were to capture the villages controlled by the Germans. Here was the essence of Simond's originality. The concept of 'armoured' infantry was itself not new, and was among the many in-

novations advocated, largely unsuccessfully, by the proponents of tank development whose views were notoriously and scandalously rejected in the inter-war years. Simonds, however, was among the first to put the idea into effect, and to do so he improvised the necessary bullet and shrapnel proof carriers by removing the 105mm guns from the 3rd Canadian Division's Priest self-propelled artillery vehicles. The gun apertures were covered with armour plating, and the vehicles, which earned the familiar name of 'unfrocked priests', were just large enough to carry an infantry section of eight men. The problem of converting enough Priests was placed in the hands of the Royal Electrical and Mechanical Engineers, who worked a minor engineering miracle comparable to the production of the Rhino Shermans for Operation Cobra. They worked day and night to complete the job on time, and despite the timing of the attack being advanced by one day, they produced, with a few American half-tracks to make up the requirement, enough vehicles to transport six infantry battalions.

The other principal difficulty was the problem of navigating, not only for the armour itself, but for the aircraft which were to provide the bombardment. Royal Air Force Bomber Command was reluctant to carry out a night bombing of the area unless they could be certain of a great degree of accuracy. On the night of 6th August an experiment was carried out on the front of the British Corps to see whether the artillery could fire 25-pounder green and red marker shells into the target area to guide the bomber navigators. The tests proved satisfactory, the night bombing was agreed, and the soldiers behind the front lines once more worked at high pressure to provide the necessary equipment in the right place in time.

As for navigating the tanks and infantry carriers, it was appreciated that in a night advance it would be no easy matter to maintain control over direction, and several expedients were tried, using a variety of aids. The general lines of advance for each column were prepared by survey, and apart from compasses in their own turrets, the leading tanks were to

'Unfrocked' Priest
Details for the Unfrocked version are not certain, so all figures quoted
are for the standard Priest except for the payload figure. *Crew:* Seven men.
Weight: 52,000 pounds. *Length:* 18 feet 5½ inches. *Maximum speed:* 25 mph.
Range: 165 miles. *Payload:* about 10 men. *Engine:* 400 hp

move on radio direction beams, with
the others closely following their tail-
lights. They also had the artillery's
coloured marker shells, tracer shells
fired from the flanks of the attacking
columns, and searchlight beams to
supplement the light of the moon
which was due to rise shortly before
midnight. While Simonds was doubt-
ful that any one of these systems
would alone be adequate, he hoped that
a combination of some few of them
might do the trick.

H-Hour for the attack was 2330
hours on 7th August, and on 5th
August Crerar, who clearly knew his
military history, briefed his senior
officers, stressing the vital nature of
operation: 'We have reached what
very much appears to be the potentially decisive period of this five-year
World War . . . Our responsibility is a
proud as well as a great one, and I
have no doubt that we shall make 8th
August 1944 an even blacker day for
the German Armies than is recorded
against that same date twenty-six

years ago.' On that day in 1918, Canadian, Australian and British soldiers
burst through the German defences
facing Amiens to a depth of eight
miles, and began the offensive which
ended in the Armistice. Ludendorff
later described 8th August 1918 as
'the black day of the German Army'.
Crerar, over optimistically – and as it
turned out with conspicuous lack of
accuracy – also predicted that the
First Canadian Army's first major
offensive action would convince the
Germans that general defeat of their
armies on all fronts had become an
inescapable fact, and that a quick
termination of the war would follow.

The formation for the attack consisted of six long, narrow columns of
tanks, together with flail tanks of the
Lothian and Border Yeomanry to
explode any mines that were encountered. The right hand four
columns, on the western side of the
Caen/Falaise road, were formed by the
2nd Canadian Armoured Brigade and
the 4th Canadian Infantry Brigade;

on the left (eastern) side of the road, the spearhead would consist of two British columns formed from the 33rd Armoured and 154th Highland Brigades. For the second phase, on the afternoon of 8th August, 4th Canadian and 1st Polish Armoured Divisions were to pass through the line gained and carry on the drive towards Falaise.

About an hour before midnight on 7th August the artillery began to mark out the target with their coloured shells, and the bombing followed from the RAF. Half an hour later, the tanks moved off on either side of the road, in a tidy, compact armoured formation, with only two yards between vehicles and four vehicles abreast, so that each column comprised a solid formation sixteen yards wide and some 350 yards long. As they crossed the start line, and settled down to a steady five miles per hour, with each tank closely following the one in front, all appeared to be going well. Then the massive rolling artillery barrage which was to precede the tanks opened up, and the entire picture suddenly changed.

To capture the atmosphere of that extraordinary night, it is worth following the fortunes of a specific unit. The activities of the 144th RAC, leading the column just to the east of the road, were typical. Its experiences were recounted in detail in the history of the unit written by the commanding officer, Lieutenant-Colonel Alan Jolly, and are quoted at length by Sir Basil Liddell Hart in his book *The Tanks*, from which the following is a summarised account:

'The moment the barrage opened the column became enveloped in a dense cloud of dust, and the notion of following the tail light of the tank in front became absurd. Worse, the leading tank in the column had heard no sound from the radio beam, and when the barrage started its compass went wild, swinging about in all directions. The tank promptly fell into a ten feet deep bomb crater, and was out of action. As if the loss of the leading tank were not enough, the two navigating tanks acting as its reserve tried to skirt the crater, and immediately fell into another.'

'From then on the confusion was scarcely describable. Some tanks crossed over the road, without even realising it, and British and Canadian vehicles became mixed up together. Tanks loomed out of the dust and darkness, and their commanders enquired helplessly of each other where they all were, though none could help the others. Nobody seemed to take any notice of the enemy, whose reaction on this unit's front seemed to be confined to bursts from a single machine-gun. Then one tank found a railway line which served as a landmark, and discovered a hut that marked their crossing point. A Verey light was fired, and other tanks began to loom out of the darkness, some of them guided by officers on foot. Suddenly, the enemy struck back. A Bazooka fired from behind the hut hit one tank and knocked it out. Another shot was more effective, and a tank 'brewed up' in flames, lighting up the scene with its macabre glow. An officer, Captain Stephens, collected a handful of men and raced off with hand grenades to deal with the Germans, and soon the enemy were quiet again.'

'Finally the barrage stopped and the dust cleared, and the tanks, hopelessly out of order but able to pick up their direction by the light of the moon, moved slowly forwards. Soon a landmark was picked out, and the leading officers fired up Verey pistols to show the way and keep what was left of the columns together. But the Verey pistols were probably more help to the enemy than to the tankers. Their coloured shells helped the Germans to pinpoint targets, and a hail of mortar fire from the *nebelwerfer* started to rain down. The column's liaison officer decided, correctly as it turned out, somewhat to everyone's astonishment, that they had arrived at the designated debussing point for the infantry. In any case, the German fire, from close range, now made it essential for the infantry to take over. They dismounted from their armoured vehicles and moved off solidly towards their first target village, Cramesnil, and at 0530 hours it was in their hands.'

This advance was fairly typical of the operation, although some units, especially on the right flank, became

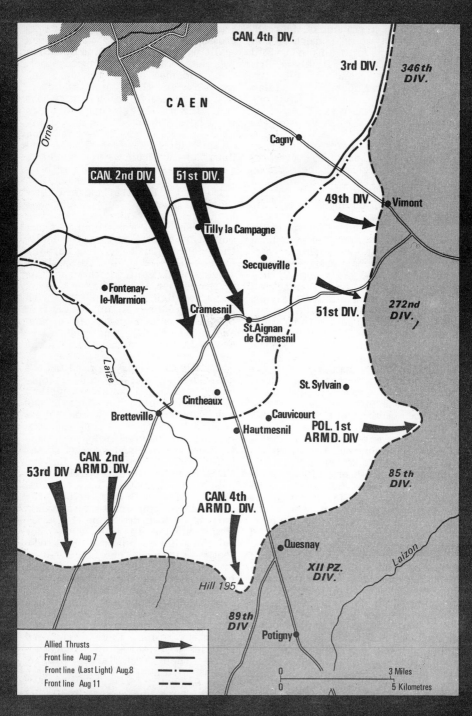

CAN. 4th DIV.

3rd DIV.

346th DIV.

CAEN

Orne

Cagny

CAN. 2nd DIV. **51st DIV.**

49th DIV.

Vimont

Tilly la Campagne

Secqueville

51st DIV.

272nd DIV.

Fontenay-le-Marmion

Cramesnil

St.Aignan de Cramesnil

Laize

St. Sylvain

Cintheaux

Cauvicourt

Bretteville

Hautmesnil

POL. 1st ARMD. DIV

53rd DIV **CAN. 2nd ARMD. DIV.**

85th DIV.

CAN. 4th ARMD. DIV.

Quesnay

Laizon

Hill 195

XII PZ. DIV.

89th DIV

Potigny

Allied Thrusts
Front line Aug 7
Front line (Last Light) Aug.8
Front line Aug 11

0   3 Miles
0   5 Kilometres

Operation Totalize

The Allied air attack. An ammunition dump goes up north of Falaise

The wait as the air bombardment goes on

Opposite page: The Canadians move south from Caen
Above: Polish tank crews prepare

The Canadian soldier may fight again:
the German tank – never

Top: German half-tracks, en route for a country battle. *Above:* The troops load their multiple rocket-launchers

even more confused and disorientated, and missed their target areas altogether. But there is no doubt that the night attack was a great success, if not in terms of ground gained, then certainly in terms of morale. And the confusion wrought in the enemy lines was total. The Germans had no idea how many tanks were engaged in the operation (one estimate mentioned 600) and early that morning parties of German infantry were streaming down the roads in search of safety. One man alone appears to have been responsible for preventing a complete rout. Major-General Kurt Meyer, 12th SS Commander, positioned himself in the middle of the road, challenged the fleeing troops, and forced them back to the positions they had abandoned in the region of Cintheaux. He also brought up twenty available tanks to reinforce the line, and recalled a further battle group of twenty tanks and 200 infantrymen which he had despatched to another sector. By noon he had ordered a counterattack against the Allies north of Cintheaux, which proved extremely successful. During the afternoon, the US Eighth Air Force bombed the area of Bretteville, Cintheaux, and St Sylvain in preparation for the second phase of the advance by the 4th Canadian and 1st Polish Armoured Divisions, but because Meyer had pushed his men forwards, towards the attackers, the main weight of the bombing fell behind them, and they were able to repulse the Polish Division, halting them in the woods south of Cramesnil.

On the right of the Poles, the Canadian armour broke through as far as Bretteville, but they too were stopped before they reached their final objectives. During daylight hours on that day, 8th August, both Poles and Canadians managed to advance only three miles, and the impetus provided by the original night attack was lost. Had these divisions not been engaged on their first action, they might have shown more determination and aggression, and realised that pockets of resistance are best dealt with by bypassing for subsequent reduction, rather than delaying the advance to indulge in immediate and time-consuming engagements. Nevertheless the Germans were still worried about the situation, and on the night of 8th August Kluge remarked: 'A breakthrough has taken place south of Caen such as we have never seen before.'

The following day, Meyer began an organised withdrawal to the River Laizon, and by 10th August the German 85th Division arrived to take over that line of defence from the depleted and shaken 12th SS Panzer Division. That night the British 144th RAC attacked to dislodge the German outposts two miles north of the River Laizon, and even though they took the positions, German shelling made any further advance impossible.

On 14th August Simonds mounted another armoured attack aimed at breaking through to Falaise, called Operation Tractable. It was similar to Operation Totalize, but this time the tanks were formed not into long lines but into solid phalanxes 250 yards square. The attack was timed on this occasion not for darkness but for noon, and the tanks used an extensive smoke-screen for cover, rather than darkness. After a heavy air and artillery bombardment, the tanks and 'unfrocked priests' carrying infantry drove straight through the German 85th Division, scattering them in disorder, and crossed the river. Finally the remnants of 12th SS Panzer Division, reduced to eleven tanks, 300 infantrymen, and a dozen 88s, held them up three miles short of Falaise, and they were still there on 16th August when Falaise was entered from the west.

Thus the Totalize and Tractable attacks, brilliantly conceived and promising an entirely novel and virtually irresistible method of overcoming a static defence, had come to grief far short of their objective.

What had gone wrong? Since the bulk of the German armour was engaged in the push to Avranches, their offensive towards Falaise might have led to the most valuable isolation of the German army in the west; but it seems that the attack was conceived and carried out without the necessary period for training in night operations. Had the troops involved been more experienced in night navigation in tanks, and had they been more familiar with the tactics involved in such an attack, keeping it going by moving constantly forward behind the enemy's main lines of defence, instead of getting bogged down in fighting for them, there is no doubt that they would have pushed through to the areas where there was virtually nothing to stop them. In the event, the enemy had time to withdraw sufficient of his forces to mount a continuing and determined defence. Falaise was finally entered by the Canadian 2nd Division on 16th August, after savage fighting. But by then bombs and shells had reduced the buildings to heaps of rubble, and the bulldozers which moved in to clear up the debris had difficulty in identifying even where the streets had been. William the Conqueror's birthplace lay in ruins.

Falaise: the killing ground

Before the first Canadian attack towards Falaise ground to a halt, the tactical aspects of the battle were beginning to take a new turn, as events took over from plans, and new patterns began to offer new opportunities.

With the US Third Army moving eastwards round the southern flank of the German concentrations, the Canadians attacking from the north, and with the Germans themselves still pushing towards Avranches, the Allied commanders began clearly to see the possibilities of diverging from the planned push towards the Seine on a wide front, and instead turning the Third Army towards the north, to meet the Canadians coming south and cut off the Germans in a vast pocket.

Patton had obviously been alert to such a possibility when he told Haislip that a turn to the north was not out of the question. Kluge had also seen the threat and after considerable soul-searching and consultations with Eberbach and Hausser, he had written to Hitler suggesting that he should call off the attack towards Avranches, and turn to the south to strike at the American salient moving north.

On 8th August General Bradley looked at the situation and came to the same conclusion: that by their attack at Mortain the Germans had incurred the threat of encirclement from the south and north. On that day, when General Eisenhower was present at his headquarters, Bradley telephoned Montgomery, and proposed that instead of driving towards the Seine, the First and Third Armies should turn to the north and attack towards Flers and Argentan. Patton's words to Haislip were at last on the point of coming true. Bradley suggested that, at the same time as the Americans moved north, the British and Canadian forces comprising the 21st Army Group should advance to the south and the two forces should meet on the army group boundary – the line running approximately east/west from the area of Mortain through Sées.

Bradley proposed to carry out this plan by turning Patton's Army north from le Mans, and also by pivoting Hodges' First Army on Mortain, so that it could attack to the northeast, in the direction of Flers. The two commanders then set about fulfilling these aggressive missions with their own detailed plans.

On 11th August, when Patton had already started his move to the north, Montgomery made known his concept of the encirclement idea. He accepted Bradley's plan for a direct attack to the north, but remained cool enough to temper the excitement of that new opportunity with a sober plan to take account of the possibility of failure. He judged that the most likely enemy reaction would be to try to hold open the closing jaws, and escape to the east, in order to retain access to their vital supply and ammunition dumps. Montgomery felt that this German reaction would render it easier for the Canadian army to capture Falaise and push on towards Argentan than it would be for the Americans to reach Argentan from the south against the defences the Germans were likely to mount. He therefore ordered the Canadians to push ahead with their attack to Falaise with all speed. Montgomery wrote with his usual restraint: 'It begins to look as if the enemy intends to fight it out between the Seine and the Loire. This will suit us very well.' At the same time, he impressed on Bradley the necessity of continuing the longer movement towards the Seine.

The objective of XV Corps, which was to carry out the drive to the north from le Mans, was set some eleven miles north of Alençon, along the road between Carrouges and Sées. Haislip, the corps commander, was ordered to lead with his 5th Armoured Division, and with the attached French 2nd Armoured Division, which, under Major-General Jacques Philippe Leclerc, had been brought from Africa especially to represent the French forces in the invasion. Offered at last their chance to take part in the liberation of their occupied country, the French promised to play an important and aggressive part in the coming operation. On 10th August the two armoured divisions moved off with the French on the left, and in the face of the piecemeal but occasionally sharp enemy defensive reaction, reached about halfway to Alençon. That night, the French troops lived

Major-General Philippe Leclerc, Commander of 2nd French Armoured Division

up to the expectations widely held for them and captured the bridges over the Sarth river at Alençon intact. On the morning of the 11th the 5th Armoured Division took the town of Sées.

On the night of 11th August the advance appeared to be going sufficiently well for Haislip to redefine the corps objective, setting his sights on Argentan, but an extraordinary and totally unexpected deficiency blotted an otherwise exemplary operation. To keep clear the road from Alençon to Argentan for the 5th Armoured Division, Haislip had instructed Leclerc to avoid allowing his armour to stray onto the road, and to keep to the left, or west, of the Forêt d'Écouve. Leclerc nevertheless took it upon himself to ignore the divisional boundaries, and disregarding Haislip's order, sent one combat command through the woods and another round them on the eastern side. This latter command caused inevitable congestion on the road and forced the 5th Armoured Division to postpone its attack for six hours, by which time an infantry battalion of 116th Panzer Division had arrived at

Mortrée and was in a position to block the American advance. It was not the last time that the French were to demonstrate their apparent inability to adhere to the agreed chain of command and obey orders.

When Kluge on 10th August had come to the conclusion that Canadian and American movements were presenting him with a real threat of envelopment, he had turned his attention away from the second attack which Hitler demanded should be carried out towards Avranches, and now wondered whether a swiftly executed thrust by the Panzers could not smash the spearhead of the columns driving north. Kluge requested that Jodl, the chief of the German Armed Forces Operations Staff, should pass his suggestion to Hitler for approval. Hitler at that stage gave no decision, but replied by asking a series of questions, mostly, it seemed, to clarify the issue for his own better understanding, but also to prevent Kluge from carrying out a manoeuvre which was less aggressive than that already planned, for at this stage he had come to regard almost all his commanders with the deepest suspicion.

After discussing the situation with his colleagues Eberbach and Hausser on 11th August, Kluge submitted a written report to Hitler, proposing that the attacking forces should be withdrawn from the Mortain area, and assembled around Carrouges for the strike against the spearheads of the advancing US Third Army. The main forces for the attack were to be the 1st SS and 2nd and 116th Panzer Divisions. Hitler at last recognised the threat to the southern flank of the army group, agreed to a minor withdrawal of the front between Sourdeval and Mortain, and approved an attack against the American armies, The decision came only just in time. When Eberbach visited the Alençon area on the afternoon of 11th August he found the defences in shreds. Allied attacks from planes and antitank guns had littered the countryside with debris, and the German troops were retreating to the north in the path of the American advance. On 12th August the XLVII Panzer Corps Headquarters arrived, took

over responsibility for the Argentan area, and moved the first Panzer battalion to arrive, part of the 116th Panzer Division, to Mortrée, where it was just in time to block the American 5th Armoured Division's advance. The remainder of 116th Panzer Division, owing to the speed and strength of the French and American advance, also had to be disposed in defence, with the result that the strike at the Allied spearheads planned by Kluge and agreed by Hitler had to be called off. The other Panzer divisions scheduled to take part in the counterattack, 1st SS and 2nd Panzer Divisions, began to reach Argentan on 13th August, and they too, though arriving in only partial strength, were compelled to take immediate defensive positions.

With the German Seventh Army and Fifth Panzer Army thus thrown continually on the defensive, the true nature of the situation at last began to dawn on the German commanders, and on 13th August Josef 'Sepp' Dietrich, the Fifth Panzer Army commander, finally committed himself to the first outright recommendation that steps should be taken to save the bulk of the Wehrmacht in the west from total destruction.

He openly warned: ' . . . if every effort is not made to move the forces toward the east and out of the threatened encirclement, the army group will have to write off both armies. Within a very short time re-supplying the troops with ammunition and fuel will no longer be possible. Therefore, immediate measures are necessary to move to the east before such movement is definitely too late. It will soon be possible for the enemy to fire into the pocket with artillery from all sides.'

Yet before either Hitler or any of the other commanders were able to react to the recommendation, events took still another unexpected turn. The American pressure towards Argentan suddenly eased, and the gap between the Americans and French south of Argentan and the Canadians in the region of Falaise remained blessedly and invitingly open. Why?

The jaws begin to close: The Canadians attack south from Falaise

Left and above: The Americans move North

Above right: Dietrich. *right:* Jodl

The destruction in the pocket begins

Why, at the moment when Montgomery's plan for defeating the enemy between the Seine and the Loire seemed on the point of coming to fruition, did they hesitate from delivering what might have been the *coup de grace* to almost the entire German army in the west? There are several reasons. Most important was the peril of allowing the two armies to press forward at great speed, with the risk of what General Eisenhower described in his book, *Crusade in Europe*, as a 'calamitous battle between friends'. Almost equally important was the extended nature of the American XV Corps's salient facing to the north, and the fact that it was exposed and vulnerable on both sides. Even if they succeeded in reaching Falaise, there was considerable doubt that they would be able to hold the pocket closed if the Germans chose, as they inevitably must, to avoid annihilation by means of a withdrawal to the east. There would be every chance of the Americans being overrun. Moreover, at this stage, the Canadians had not yet started their second attack towards Falaise, and Montgomery did not yet know that heavy defences were deployed against the northern 'pincer'. At that time, it seemed entirely proper that the task of closing the gap should devolve on the Canadians and British converging on Falaise from the north.

Lastly, there was, once again, the question of broad strategy. And this depended on Montgomery, who while holding now only the same position as Bradley as an army group commander, was nevertheless (pending Eisenhower's taking over command himself) effectively in command of the Allied ground forces in Europe. And in Montgomery's plan the American attack to the north from le Mans was still, in a sense, a secondary concept, the more important movement being the wider advance of Third Army eastward towards the Seine. The decision to retain the position of the army group boundary, not to allow the Americans to proceed to the north of it, and rely on the still unlaunched second Canadian attack, therefore stood: but it angered the Americans then and continued to do so well after

the war.

While it is pointless and in bad taste to over-emphasise the wrangling and bitterness which showed in the various post-war accounts given by the commanders involved, it is worthwhile, in order to set the record straight, recalling Bradley's words, to the effect that the 'shocked Third Army looked on helplessly as its quarry fled', and that 'Patton raged at Montgomery's blunder'. Patton even told Bradley: 'Let me go on to Falaise and we'll drive the British back into the sea for another Dunkirk.'

Eisenhower later claimed that had the gap been closed then the Allies might have won a complete battle of annihilation. Once more, however, it must be stressed that these are the words of hindsight. At the time the exact nature and strength of the German forces in the pocket were not clear to Montgomery. Intelligence estimates had indicated that some of the Germans had already escaped from the pocket, although these reports turned out to be incorrect, and Montgomery's wider thrust was calculated to round up and destroy both those who had supposedly escaped, and those who had never been in the pocket in the first place, but who were located anywhere between the Seine and Loire west of the Paris-Orleans gap.

And it was these Germans, not the British, whom Montgomery was interested in destroying, so while Patton raged on the original plan stood. Indeed, when it was modified, to re-dispose the troops for the next phase, the plan veered even further away from a northern thrust to close the gap, and put increased emphasis on the eastward push.

When Bradley halted the advance of XV Corps on 13th August, the German command had still not decided on a withdrawal, despite the threat of encirclement. And on 14th August a new order from Hitler called for an attack in Eberbach's sector in the Alençon–Carrouges area to destroy part of the American XV Corps, using the 9th and 10th SS Panzer Divisions and the 21st Panzer Division. Hitler attributed the perilous situation in the rear of the army group to the failure of the first attack on Av-

The Germans try to plot a coherent escape

ranches, and warned that Panzer Group Eberbach, because it was committed too far to the north, would become involved in a sterile frontal fight.

But once more the realities of the situation rendered Hitler's orders obsolete. When on 14th August Kluge went to visit Dietrich's Fifth Panzer Army he found appalling problems. There was far from sufficient strength to react to the Canadian attack, and 21st Panzer Division had to be diverted to Falaise to reinforce the defences there. At the same time, Kluge was informed that on the southern sector 10th SS Panzer Division was engaged with the Americans in the region of Domfront.

Thus only the 9th SS Panzer Division, of the three designated by Hitler for the assault, was available. On 15th August a new complication arose: Kluge vanished. He left Dietrich's headquarters to see Eberbach and Hausser, but never arrived. Nobody could contact him anywhere, and his staff were plunged into confusion. On the evening of 15th August, Blumentritt, Kluge's chief of staff, talked with Jodl on the telephone, pointed out the perilous state of affairs, and reiterated the contention of Hausser, Dietrich, and Eberbach that a decision to withdraw was needed quickly. He also stressed that with the battle at a critical stage, Hitler should appoint a replacement for Kluge immediately. Within the hour, Hitler had appointed Hausser as acting commander of Army Group B, with the mission of attacking and destroying the American forces near Sées which threatened to encircle the armies in the west – Fifth Panzer Army, Seventh Army, and Panzer Group Eberbach.

The mystery of Kluge's disappearance, however, was solved on the evening of 15th August when he turned up. He had apparently been in a car which was spotted and attacked by an Allied aircraft. His radio was smashed, and he was forced to take cover in a ditch, which he could not leave until after dark because of the aircraft overhead. Later that month Hitler, at a conference, openly accused Kluge of having been 'missing' in order to make contact with the Allies with a view of surrending the whole of the western army and going over to the enemy himself. Hitler added: '15th August was the worst day of my life. It was due only to an accident that the plan (for surrender) was not carried out. The measures taken by the Army Group cannot be explained except in the light of this assumption.'

It should be made clear that the Allies, after the war, could produce no evidence to show that Kluge had been trying to contact them, and that when he turned up, Eberbach described him as being 'very shaken' which appears to be more consistent with a nasty combat experience than with an unsuccessful attempt to capitulate.

As early as 0200 hours on the morning of 16th August Kluge, back at Dietrich's headquarters, informed Jodl that from what he had seen it was impossible to amass sufficient armour for the proposed attack to the southeast, and he frankly recommended that the western armies threatened with encirclement should mount an immediate withdrawal through the Argentan-Falaise gap while it still remained open. Shortly after mid-day he again telephoned Jodl, and this time secured an admission from Jodl that a withdrawal to the east was vital. Jodl, however, still not completely in touch with the situation, demanded that the attack to the south-east should go ahead, to enlarge the escape opening and form a well-defended 'hard shoulder' to protect the withdrawing forces.

Kluge's reply was unequivocal: 'No matter how many orders are issued, the troops cannot, are not able to, are not strong enough to defend against

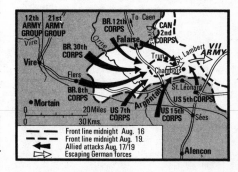

Battle of the pocket

the enemy. It would be a fateful error to succumb to a hope that cannot be fulfilled, and no power in this world can accomplish its will simply through an order it may give. This is the situation.'

Jodl at last promised that a concise and clear directive from the Führer would be sent to Kluge as quickly as possible. Anticipating its contents, Kluge began to organise the withdrawal, issuing orders that it should take place on the following two nights, across the Orne river. When Hitler's directive did arrive, it went further, and authorised a withdrawal behind the Dives river further to the east. But Jodl had obviously had a hand in forming the order and it called again for an attack to enlarge the escape corridor, and insisted that Falaise should be held in strength as a northern 'corner pillar'. While Jodl and Hitler seemed still determined to ignore the fact that there were no resources with which to fulfil these conditions, the withdrawal began on the night of 16th August.

The Germans planned to move their forces out of the pocket in three overnight moves, beginning on 16th August. The first phase of the withdrawal, back to the Orne river, was carried out with comparatively few problems, since the Allies restrained from interfering. But on 17th August Montgomery issued an uncompromising order, which changed the whole situation. It was absolutely essential, he said, to close the gap. The two armoured divisions of 2nd Canadian Corps, 4th Canadian and 1st Polish Armoured Divisions, were to attack through Trun and push on to Chambois as quickly as possible.

Also on 17th August came an important change in the command structure of the German armies, when Field-Marshal Walter Model arrived from the Eastern Front to take over as commander of Army Group B. Until Model became familiar with the situation, Kluge was nominally to retain the post, but he was ordered to keep out of the pocket. For Kluge, who had fought to protect the troops under him, and had done his best to impress on his Führer the realities of a quickly deteriorating situation, it was an ignominious end. Kluge had been a perfectly honourable soldier, but he had found increasing difficulty in resolving the conflict, which at some time appears to perplex so many soldiers, between his professional military opinion, and obedience to his superiors, who may also be the civilian government, as Hitler was. Shortly before he was relieved Kluge had said to a colleague 'You may rest assured that I shall talk with him [Hitler] again tonight without mincing any words. Something has to happen. I owe this to the troops and to the German people, one way or another.' Kluge then composed a letter to the Führer stating unequivocally his view on recent events, and it is worth quoting extensively to illustrate the continuing rift between Hitler and his generals.

'When you receive these lines, I shall be no more. I cannot bear the accusation that I sealed the fate of the West by taking wrong measures . . . I have been relieved of command. The evident reason is the failure of the armoured units in their push to Avranches and the consequent impossibility of closing the gap to the sea. As responsible commander, my 'guilt' is thereby affirmed. Allow me, my Führer, to state my position in all deference.'

Kluge went on to say that the order to drive to the north from Avranches in an attempt to change the strategic situation in the west had been completely out of the question, and that the order presupposed a state of affairs that did not exist.

'Should the new weapons in which you place so much hope, especially those of the air force, not bring success . . . then, my Führer, make up your mind to end the war. The German people have suffered so unspeakably that it is time to bring the horror to a close . . .'

'I have steadfastly stood in awe of your greatness, your bearing in this gigantic struggle, and your iron will . . . If Fate is stronger than your will and your genius, that is Destiny. You have made an honourable and tremendous fight. History will testify this for you. Show now that greatness that will be necessary if it comes to the point of ending a struggle which has become hopeless.'

'I depart from you, my Führer, having stood closer to you in spirit than you perhaps dreamed, in the consciousness of having done my duty to the utmost.'

On 19th August Kluge set out by car for Germany, but he never arrived. Before the car reached Metz he was dead. Apparently he had swallowed a phial of potassium cyanide, although the doctor who examined his body reported that he had died of a cerebral haemorrhage. Hitler at first ordered a state funeral and invited Rundstedt to deliver a funeral oration on his behalf, but on receiving Kluge's letter he cancelled the ceremony, and Kluge was buried quietly at home with no public acclamation.

Much as they had reason to be grateful for Kluge's efforts on their behalf, the troops in the pocket had in their new commander a man who not only worked hard to save them, but who was in a position to do so without being perpetually suspected and without having his views constantly frustrated. Model had long been one of Hitler's favourites, and had been promoted rapidly through the officer hierarchy to achieve the rank of field-marshal at the age of only fifty-four. He was not born into one of Germany's officer producing families, but was very much a 'self-made man', and for that reason he was not tied down by the hidebound ideas of German military thinking. Hitler, not a member of the German aristocracy himself, preferred Model's aggressive, ruthless, and professional outlook to that of the traditional officer classes, and Model had fully vindicated Hitler's faith in him by his record of aggression and resourcefulness in Russia in 1941 and 1942, both as leader of a Panzer division and as an army commander. In 1943 he had survived a serious setback when the German forces were defeated in the battle of the Kursk salient, a defeat attributable to Hitler's preference for Model's plans over those of Kluge and Manstein. Later that year he had restored his fortunes with such a series of successes in bringing Russian offensives to a halt that Hitler called him the saviour of the Eastern Front, and regarded him as a brilliant defensive strategist. Thus he had remained

Field-Marshal Model, who took over command in the west

Hitler's favourite, and, surprisingly perhaps, was the one general brave enough to stand up to Hitler and back his own views. Possibly his confidence and freedom from suspicion were based on the fact that he was the first of the generals on the Eastern Front to confirm his allegiance to the Führer after the 20th July attempt on Hitler's life.

Model's reaction to the situation he found on his arrival in the West was characteristically vigorous. He conferred with the commanders on the spot on 18th August, and as a result dropped all ideas of counterattacks. He began to draw up plans not simply to withdraw to the Orne river, nor even just to the Dives, but for a withdrawal, by the night of 20th August, to the Touques river, running from Gacé to Lisieux some twenty miles east of Falaise. Uncompromisingly, he was getting right out of the pocket, Model proposed that after this withdrawal, the Seventh Army was to take over the defence of the sector from Laigle to the sea, and Fifth Panzer Army that between Laigle and Paris. First Army, now on the move from the south of France, was designated for the defence of the Paris sector and the reaches of the Seine above the capital. Thus, immediately on Model's arrival, there entered into German thinking that same general issue, a co-ordinated withdrawal, against which Hitler had been so firmly set, and over which Kluge had been humiliated and sacrificed. Kluge's son, himself fighting in the pocket, might well have wondered at the current state of justice in the German army. Most important, Model stressed that the withdrawal could not be achieved without hard fighting, and that since the troops were exhausted, no great efforts could be expected from them. Consequently, he requested immediately twenty-five replacement battalions, 270 tanks or assault-guns, nine artillery battalions, and as many howitzers as possible, as well as the dispatch to the western front of six further Panzer brigades now being formed in Germany.

During the critical phase when these changes were taking place in the German command, the Allies had not of course been standing idly by. In response to Montgomery's order to close the gap, on 17th August 4th Canadian Armoured Division, side-stepping the German defences at Falaise, broke across the Dives river at Morteaux-Coulibeuf, and swept onwards to the south east. The Canadians captured Trun, and sent reconnaisance parties as far as St Lambert. Meanwhile forward units of 1st Polish Armoured Division reached to within half a mile of Chambois. Thus one road by which the Germans might plan to escape from the pocket, through Trun, was closed to them, and the other one, through Chambois, was now under fire.

On the southern jaw, on 18th August, the V Corps, under the command of General Gerow, attacked north from le Bourg St Leonard, and reached halfway to Chambois before they were stopped. The escape route from the pocket was thus reduced to only about five miles width. During that night for the first time, the Allies started to pound the pocket with artillery fire, and at daybreak on 19th August Allied planes added their weight to the attack with bombing

Hawker Typhoon IB
Engine: Napier Sabre IIA, 2,180 hp *Armament:* Four 20mm Hispano cannon and eight 3-inch rockets or two 1,000 lb bombs *Maximum Speed:* 404 mph at 10,000 feet *Ceiling:* 34,000 feet *Range:* 374 miles with max fuel *Weight empty:* 8,280 lbs *Weight loaded:* 11,700 lbs *Span:* 41 feet 7 inches *Length:* 31 feet 10 inches

The FFI greet the British

and strafing runs. The Germans suffered a terrible onslaught, and there was little by way of cover. Withdrawing in the face of this attack, Seventh Army and Panzer Group Eberbach had by the night of 19th August fallen back to behind the railway running north from Argentan and off to the east of Falaise, so that that the pocket itself was then only six miles wide. Inside it, compressed to provide the Allies with an even easier target, were the remains of some fifteen fighting divisions, together with innumerable service troops, stragglers, isolated units, and an unaccountable quantity of tanks, guns, supply trains, and other equipment.

By 19th August, the situation had developed to the point where Hausser, whom Model had placed in charge of all the forces still within the pocket, deemed it imperative to get at least across the Dives river that night, before the Allied thrusts at Trun and Chambois closed them in altogether. Visiting as many of the corps headquarters as possible, Hausser spent all day on 19th August planning and preparing for the breakout from the pocket. His idea was for II Parachute Corps and XLVII Panzer Corps to attack across the Dives river side by side, while II SS Panzer Corps would attack from the outside into the pocket to open up the way for the Seventh Army and Panzer Group Eberbach escape. In the event, this last attack could not be mounted that night and II Parachute Corps and XLVII Panzer Corps were compelled to make the breakout themselves.

And while Hausser laid his plans, the pocket contracted even further. In the west, British troops crossed the Orne river and reached almost to the Falaise/Argentan road; 4th Canadian Armoured Division in the north extended its salient with a push as far as St Lambert; and 1st Polish Division went south-east, and after some sharp fighting secured a prominent and valuable position known as Hill 262 overlooking the Chambois Vimoutiers road. Another detachment of the Polish Division moved directly south and entered Chambois from the north, where they met American troops of General Gerow's 90th Division, who had moved into the town from the south, Thus, as the two jaws met, the pocket was closed.

Now, instead of having to escape between the two Allied forces, the Germans would have to break through the Allied lines. Fortunately the cordon the Allies had thrown around the Germans, although continuous, was thin, and there seemed at least a fair prospect of being able to creep through it, if not fight out of it. And the German troops were in good heart at last: they had been given orders to withdraw, and a fighting chance was infinitely preferable to sitting around acting as targets for Allied artillery and bomb-aiming practice. Any tendency to be disheartened which might have remained was dispelled by determined commanders like Lieutenant-General Richard Schimpf, who told his own 3rd Parachute Division that false rumours were like bad odours, since both came from the rear, and admonished them for worrying that their supply lines might be temporarily cut off. He told them that there was 'no reason for a paratrooper, who is specially trained to jump into the midst of the enemy, to feel depressed. He who thinks or talks otherwise will be slapped across the mouth.'

Shortly before midnight, the escape began, and from then on, with communications almost non-existent, individual units struggled eastwards independently. Some succeeded, some failed, but almost all who escaped did so only after daring exploits. One of the most interesting adventures was that of a small group from 3rd Parachute Division. Schimpf, their commander, was severely wounded, and the commander of II Parachute Corps, General Eugen Meindl, took over responsibility for them. By the time they reached the Dives river, however, he had lost contact with most of the paratroops, and only had about twenty left. In the course of searching for a suitable crossing place over the Dives, they encountered another regimental commander who told them of a ford between Trun and Chambois. They waded over, avoided three tanks sitting on the skyline on a hill, and were ambushed by machine-gun fire from another tank. They flung themselves to the ground, but

General Eugen Meindl, successful evader in the pocket

the three tanks on the hill also opened fire, killing several men and reducing Meindl's party to fifteen. Fortunately, the Allies were over-fond of using tracer bullets, and the Germans managed to crawl along the furrows in the fields, and make for the obvious gaps between firing positions

At daybreak, Meindl found himself witnessing German attacks on the Polish position on Hill 262, attacks which were easily stopped by devastating fire from the Poles. Meindl decided to try to take the hill from the north, and set off to locate the Seventh Army commander, Hausser Together they formulated a plan to use the available troops and Panzers for the breakout in that region, and throughout the day the Germans mounted as series of desperate attacks against the Polish positions. After a bitter and bloody battle, the Poles remained in possession of the hill, but their perimeter was so reduced that the Germans held control at last of some of the escape roads in the area.

Along one of them, to Champosoult, there took place one of the strangest and most heartening examples of how the chivalry of war can show through even in the bloodiest and bitterest of conflicts. Meindl, anxious to protect the wounded, of whom there were all too many, halted all traffic along the road for fifteen minutes to alert the Allies to his intentions. He organised a column of trucks in close and therefore vulnerable formation, marked them with clear red crosses, and sent them out under the muzzles of the Allied guns to carry the wounded out of the pocket. Fortunately, the Allies got the message, and held their fire until the column was safely out of the way. Then they opened up again and resumed the slaughter. Meindl later acknowledged 'a feeling of gratitude to the chivalrous enemy'.

Late into that night, 20th August, the dash eastwards went on, until Meindl at last learned from the rearguard of a Panzer division that no more troops were following. Meindl himself stayed awake that night in the pouring rain, while his men snatched a few hours sleep amid the noise and stench of the battle. At 0230 hours, he started to go round shaking the men awake, making them understand, through the haze of their early morning exhaustion, that if they were to escape at all, they had to move now. At 0345 they were all ready, and began to move off into the pouring rain. An hour and a quarter after the first men moved out, Meindl led the rearguard towards Champosoult. Two hours later they were safely out of the pocket.

Experiences like that of Meindl and the men with him were repeated up and down the line. Isolated groups, broken away from their parent units, and often picked up and led by strange officers, flooded eastwards.

At one time it looked as if the mass exodus might overrun the 1st Polish Armoured Division troops on Mont Ormel and the Americans and Poles in Chambois. There the Poles were cut off from their supply line for long periods, and had to depend at times on the charity of their American colleagues for ammunition, petrol, and food: the Americans were unsparingly generous, and the Poles later paid

warm tribute to their 'fraternity of arms'. On Mont Ormel, the Germans seemed absolutely determined to dislodge the Poles, and on 21st August mounted an almost absurdly suicidal attack up the hill, which ended with scores of German infantrymen dying in a barrage of fire from Polish machine-guns.

The Canadians, also, suffered heavily at the hands of the Germans trying desperately to keep open their escape routes to the east. In the village of St Lambert, a small force of the Canadian 4th Armoured Division had taken up positions on 19th August. Getting into the village had been no easy matter. The Canadians, together with tanks and self-propelled anti-tank guns, were commanded by Major D V Currie of the 29th Canadian Armoured Reconnaissance Regiment. Two of their tanks were knocked out immediately they set foot in the village on the evening of 18th August and the initial attack was brought to a halt. As darkness fell, Major Currie moved into the village alone, got to the two disabled tanks, and brought out the crews, despite being subjected to heavy mortar fire. He also reconnoitred the enemy positions before returning to his men. The next morning he led them back into the village, and this time, even though the Germans tried to fight them off with all the infantry and artillery they could muster, the Canadians reached the middle of St Lambert and built up defensive positions. All that day and throughout the next the Germans, in a concerted effort to keep open their escape route to the north-east, mounted fierce counterattacks, but by the evening of 20th August they had failed to dislodge the Canadians and their resources were spent. As the attack eased off, Currie, not content with having protected his now defensive positions, led his men in a further offensive to complete the capture of the entire village. In three days of exhausting fighting, Currie and his small force had not only denied a valuable escape route to the Germans, but had inflicted severe losses on the enemy, including 300 killed, 500

The Allied air forces have done their work

wounded, and over 2,000 taken prisoner. They had also destroyed seven enemy tanks and twelve 88mm guns. For his leadership and valour in the battle for St Lambert, Major Currie was awarded the British Commonwealth's highest military award, the Victoria Cross.

But generally, the battle for the pocket was fought by the Allies with air and artillery, and despite a steady trickle of escaping Germans to the east, inspired by such creditable leadership as that of Meindl, there is no doubt that the Allies gained, and retained, the upper hand.

As early as 18th August reports coming in from the bomber pilots painted a clear and graphic picture of the destruction in the area. One pilot reported that the whole area was burning. Another said that the columns of transport jammed the main roads and piled up in havoc on the side roads until they formed patterns 'like herring bones' and presented an abundance of perfect and more or less stationary targets. Also in the air in those terrible days were the little artillery spotter planes, which seemed to the Germans on the ground to hang in the air, tantalisingly out of reach, but which were so deadly in the task they fulfilled. As a result of their target reports, the artillery brought to bear accurate fire, and every few minutes a triumphant cheer would rise as the American troops saw enemy tanks, trucks, artillery pieces, even horses, disintegrate and disappear in an explosion of smoke and dust and flame. And it was the horses who contributed most to the confusion. For astonishing, cruel, and foolish as it may seem, even at this late stage in a war, when the value of mechanisation was beyond doubt, the Wehrmacht still used horses to draw the bulk of its transport and artillery. As the bombardment fell on and around the horses, they inevitably panicked, careered off the roads into fields, got tangled in their harness, or just got wounded or killed alongside the soldiers they worked with, leaving stranded guns and vehicles on the roads to block progress even more. As the battle wore on their terrified screaming gradually ceased, and every lane and field was littered with the

The battle of the pocket is over

bodies of horses and soldiers together. It was not a pretty sight. It was certainly an unforgettable one. The sober operations report of the US First Army described the carnage of the final days as perhaps the greatest of the war. It said: 'the roads and fields were littered with thousands of enemy dead and wounded, wrecked and burning vehicles, smashed artillery pieces, cars laden with the loot of France overturned and smouldering, dead horses and cattle swelling in the summer's heat.'

One officer who was well qualified to judge the extent of the carnage here was a veteran who had been in the line in the First World War, and had witnessed the battles of Aisne-Marne, St Mihiel, and Meuse-Argonne, and had then fought at St Lô only a month earlier, when that town was utterly destroyed in the desperate fighting to build up the bridgehead. He reported that even those experiences did not compare with this battle, in which the peaceful setting of the Normandy countryside 'framed a picture of destruction so great that it cannot be described.'

'I stood in a lane, surrounded by twenty or thirty dead horses or parts of horses, most of them still hitched to their wagons and carts . . . As far as my eye could reach on every line of sight, there were vehicles, wagons, tanks, guns, prime movers, sedans, rolling kitchens, etc., in various stages of destruction . . .'

'I saw no foxholes or any other type of shelter or field fortifications. The Germans were trying to run and had no place to run. They were probably too exhausted to dig . . . They were probably too tired even to surrender.'

'I left this area rather regretting I'd seen it . . . Under such conditions there are no supermen – all men become rabbits looking for a hole.'

By the afternoon of 21st August, there were no more Germans left to run. Apart from a few stragglers, they had either escaped, or had been killed or captured. The German army had suffered its greatest defeat since the Battle of Stalingrad. Yet it was not a total defeat. In the battle for the Argentan-Falaise pocket 50,000 German soldiers were taken prisoner. Another 10,000 were killed on the battlefield. But large numbers of others escaped. The exact numbers are still obscure and impossible accurately to compute. Estimates have set the figure at between 20,000 and 40,000 men, and it is unlikely that any more precise assessment can ever be made. But the numbers themselves do not tell the whole story. Many of those who escaped were supply and service troops, not élite fighting men. More significantly, they escaped with hardly any of their equipment. Tanks and artillery pieces fired until their ammunition ran out, then were abandoned owing to lack of fuel, while the men who operated them made off on foot. Smaller equipment such as radios, machine-guns, and supplies were also lost in large quantities. On the other hand, most of the commanders got away. Meindl escaped with his paratroops. Hauser was severely wounded, but his staff stayed loyal and he reached safety. Meyer, commander of 12th SS, was guided to safety by a Frenchman. Funck, the commander of XLVII Panzer Corps, took over Seventh Army from the wounded Hausser and escaped.

Thus the question remained; would it have been possible to prevent one third of the Seventh Army from getting out of the pocket? Possibly the Canadians could have moved faster and more aggressively in their thrusts southwards. Possibly Montgomery could have ordered the Americans to go on north all the way to Falaise. Perhaps, on the other hand, if the Germans had seen themselves being cut off earlier and in greater strength, they might have taken steps to escape from the pocket all the sooner. On questions of this scale, it is pointless to play with history. Certainly the participants were far too busy for post-mortems, for even while the battle for the pocket was taking place, the American XV Corps was carrying out its 'long hook' and driving fast for the Seine and Paris.

Paris: the goal

Drive to the Seine

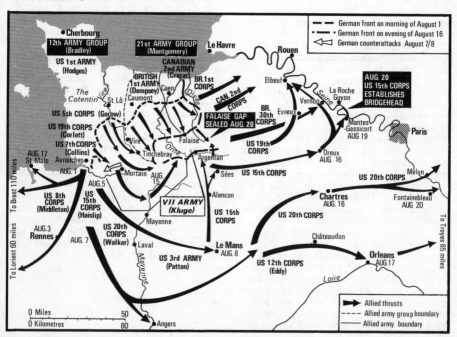

Legend:
- – – – German front on morning of August 1
- – · – German front on evening of August 16
- ◁ German counterattacks August 7/8

Cherbourg
12th ARMY GROUP (Bradley)
US 1st ARMY (Hodges)

21st ARMY GROUP (Montgomery)
Le Havre
CANADIAN 2nd ARMY (Crerar)
BRITISH 1st ARMY (Dempsey)
Caen
Caumont
BR.1st CORPS
CAN 2nd CORPS
BR.30th CORPS

Rouen
Elbeuf
La Roche Guyon
Seine
Vernon

AUG. 20 US 15th CORPS ESTABLISHES BRIDGEHEAD

The Cotentin
St.Lô
US 5th CORPS (Gerow)
US 19th CORPS (Corlett)
US 7th CORPS (Collins)
Vire
Tinchebray
Falaise
FALAISE GAP SEALED AUG.20
Argentan
Evreux
Mantes -Gassicort AUG 19
Paris

AUG.17 St-Malo
Avranches
AUG. 1
Mortain
AUG. 15
US 19th CORPS
Dreux AUG. 16
US 15th CORPS
Sées
Mélun

To Brest 110 miles
To Lorient 60 miles
AUG.5
US 8th CORPS (Middleton)
US 15th CORPS (Haislip)
US 20th CORPS (Walker)
Alencon
VII ARMY (Kluge)
US 15th CORPS
Chartres AUG. 16
US 20th CORPS
Fontainebleau AUG 20
To Troyes 65 miles

AUG.3 Rennes
AUG. 7
Mayenne
Laval
Mayenne
Le Mans AUG. 8
US 3rd ARMY (Patton)
Châteaudun
US 12th CORPS (Eddy)
Orleans AUG.17
Loire

0 Miles 50
0 Kilometres 80
Angers

Legend:
- ► Allied thrusts
- – – – Allied army group boundary
- —— Allied army boundary

The results of Montgomery's decision to continue his 'long hook' towards the Seine, even while part of the American Third Army was striking north to close the gap, became apparent while the battle for the Falaise pocket was still at its height.

In mid-August, US Third Army, facing the plain between the Seine and Loire rivers, was in an excellent position to move in behind the Germans who either escaped from the pocket or who had been outside it, and to cut off their retreat either to the Seine itself, or through the Paris/Orleans gap. Three of Patton's corps were accordingly disposed for further exploitation: XII Corps in the south was to capture Orleans, XX Corps was to take Chartres, and XV Corps was to establish a bridgehead over the River Eure at Dreux. Once again, Patton's forces exhibited all the speed and aggression which had won for them, and for Patton himself, their colourful reputation.

Under Major-General Gilbert R. Cook, XII Corps, headed by a Combat Command of 4th Armoured Division, moved off from Le Mans down the road to Orleans on 15th August. The armour was operating more or less blind, since there had been little time to carry out reconnaissance, they possessed hardly any maps of the region, and they had no idea of enemy dispositions. But they forged ahead with scant regard for caution, and on this occasion Cook's boldness exceeded even that of his army commander. They reached the outskirts of Orleans and took the airport by dusk on the first day of the advance. Cook was then ordered to halt his advance to take Châteaudun, thirty miles behind them back towards Le Mans. Cook protested vigorously, claiming that he could take both Orleans and Châteaudun, and after a further exchange of orders and protests, Patton consented to let Cook exercise his own judgement. Cook's confidence was fully justified. He mounted two converging attacks on Orleans, and on the night of 16th the city was in American hands. By noon on 17th the 320th Infantry, after an overnight march and a brief engagement with the Germans, had taken Châteaudun.

And Bayerlein, commander of Panzer Lehr, had written in an apprecia-tion at the end of June: 'A successful break-in by the enemy is never exploited to pursuit.'

The XX Corps began the drive to the Seine with the mission of taking Dreux, but when a confusion between XV and XX Corps appeared inevitable, the latter was ordered, on 14th August, to alter the objective to Chartres. Two combat commands of 7th Armoured Division reached the town on the evening of 15th August and attacked on converging lines, but they met with surprisingly strong resistance and were forced to withdraw. Part of their problem was the lack of artillery support, due not to any logistical deficiency, but to American considerateness which caused them to dispense with a bombardment in order to protect the historic town and its cathedral. After another, and only partially successful, attack on 16th August, the artillery finally commenced firing on 17th August. But the Germans still refused to give way, and it was obvious that the armour alone, in the narrow confines of the streets of Chartres, would be unable to clear the area. The 5th Division was ordered to join the attack, and on 18th August the infantry and armour together took the town, with a tally of over 2,000 prisoners to transport back to the prisoner of war cages.

On XX Corp's left, XV Corps had a much easier time in its approach to Dreux. Its 5th Armoured Division reached the Eure river on 16th August, and soon encircled Dreux. The 79th Infantry Division, advancing sixty miles in only eleven hours, had established a bridgehead over the Eure at Nogent-le-Roi, and reported no contact with the enemy.

Patton halted the three corps on 16th August on the line Orleans/Chartres/Dreux and it was the speed of the advance itself which forced him to stop his troops. The consumption of fuel in such a fast cross-country move had outstripped the available supplies, and it was becoming more and more difficult to feed the forward units along such long lines of communication. The situation was alleviated by a plan to drop supplies to the Third Army from the air. In the first of many daily drops on 19th August, forty-seven tons of rations were delivered by

Above: The magnificent cathedral at Chartres, spared the Allied bombardment. Below: It was a wise commander who had one man looking behind. Opposite page: The French join in liberating their country. FFI members are issued with British weapons

twenty-one C-47 supply aircraft near Le Mans. Almost equally important in the halting of the advance was the recurring problem of the exposed flank, and Bradley was anxious not to move too far forward until he was certain that the Third Army's northern flank would be adequately protected by the First Army advance on their left.

After only a short pause, however, these considerations were outweighed by the temptations of driving on to the Seine river only twenty-five miles away, where they could turn north, advance down the left bank of the Seine between Paris and the sea, and complete the encirclement of those German troops who might have escaped from the shorter encirclement north of Argentan. Patton and Hodges met Bradley on 17th August and Bradley ordered the advance to go on, and Patton's plan for Third Army took account of the supply difficulties. The XII Corps was to remain at Orleans, to economise on fuel, and XX Corps would take over responsibility for Dreux from XV Corps. The XV Corps itself was to advance to the Seine at Mantes-Gassicourt, thirty miles below Paris, and the advance turned out to be all too easy. The 5th Armoured and 79th Infantry Divisions reached the town on 18th August, entered it the following day, and found the Germans had departed.

It was obviously tempting to cross the river immediately and press on, but there was some delay before that could be done. Until only a few days previously, it had been intended that the Allies should halt at the Seine for some weeks, at least until the problems presented by the lack of port facilities was solved. But on 17th August Eisenhower put forward the view that the beating the enemy was receiving in Normandy would enable the Allies to dash across the Seine. By 20th August the Allied command would be thinking in terms of their next goal, the Rhine. However, there was still the prospect of finishing the job that was started in the Argentan-Falaise pocket, and it was estimated that if the Allies turned to the northwest and moved back along the left bank of the Seine, they could encircle and destroy some 75,000 more enemy

Here stood the town of Domfront

The Allies reach the Seine. Royal Engineers construct a pontoon bridge

troops. It was therefore decided that the Americans should carry out this manoeuvre, even though it meant crossing the army boundaries and moving into the British sector of advance, with all the consequent administrative problems and confusion which that move might entail.

A great deal of surprisingly hard fighting was to follow, not because the Germans were intent on defending the area, but because individual commanders mounted strong rearguard defences to protect the withdrawal to the Seine ferry crossings. The Germans had excellent cover among the ravines and woods which covered the landscape in the bends of the lower Seine, and finding extra protection in the fog and rain, small parties with *Panzerfaust* bazookas and anti-tank grenades laid ambushes for the Americans. The advance slowed down, and it was not until 24th August that they reached the vicinity of Elbeuf and Louviers. At the same time, while the Polish Armoured Division and three Canadian divisions were left to complete the slaughter in the Argentan-Falaise pocket, British Second Army

and the remainder of Canadian First Army, pushing eastwards on the coastal sector, were helping to squeeze the Germans into a second pocket, bounded by the sea and the lower reaches of the Seine.

Only one bridge was left standing, at Rouen, and as that was badly damaged the remnants of Seventh Army and Fifth Panzer Army were forced to cross the river as best they could. Some made the crossing in small boats, others on improvised rafts made from logs or even from barrels commandeered from French inns. Most managed on the ferry crossings, and were helped by the weather, which at least limited the air bombardment the Allied Air Forces mounted against the troops waiting for their turn to cross.

The majority of the Germans thus escaped across the Seine, but they left their equipment behind. Guns, tanks, and vehicles were abandoned, and only small arms taken, so that when the time came to form the survivors into new divisions on the other side of the river, there were no heavy weapons to equip them. When the losses were finally counted, out of 2,300 German

assault-guns and tanks which fought in the battle of Normandy, less than 120 were withdrawn across the Seine. General Dietrich, who was in charge of the withdrawal, said later that from the point of view of equipment abandoned, the Seine crossing was almost as great a disaster as the Falaise pocket.

While the remainder of XV Corps was beginning its move along the south bank of the Seine, 79th Division, under Major-General I T Wyche, was ordered to go ahead and cross the river at Mantes-Gassicourt, and establish a bridgehead for future operations.

The order reached 79th Division at 2135 on 19th August, when the troops had already settled down for a night's rest in Mantes. Wyche roused his men from their blankets, and in torrential rain 313th Infantry crossed the river on foot, over a dam that offered the only dry crossing in the area, each man holding on to the shoulder of the man in front to avoid falling into the river. On the 20th, 314th Infantry followed, wading across, and 315th Infantry that after-noon joined them on the far bank, crossing a hastily erected bridge. The 79th Division had not only established its bridgehead, but as a bonus succeed-ed in capturing the German Army Group B Headquarters – Rommel's former HQ – at La Roche-Guyon.

On 21st August, XX Corps and XII Corps got under way again, with attacks eastwards from Dreux and Châteaudun respectively, with the ob-ject of reaching the Seine above Paris. In another fast move which took the German defenders completely off their guard, XII Corps' Combat Command A raced to Sens and took the city that afternoon. By the following morning it had established a bridgehead over the Yonne river. By 25th August it had raced on to Troyes, another forty miles further forwards on the Seine, and after a sharp overnight fight it was across the river.

On the left of XII Corps, XX Corps was equally successful. The 5th Division's primary objective was Fontainebleau, and after an advance of forty miles on 21st August the 11th Infantry, leading the division, were stopped by a counterattack on 22nd. By the next morning, however, the defending Germans had withdrawn to the Seine, and 11th Infantry was able to cover the last twelve miles by noon. Its first crossing was distinguished by conspicuous gallantry on the part of two officers and a sergeant. One of the officers, a battalion commander, swam across the river and brought back five small boats for his men to use. The other two found a canoe on the western bank, paddled it across to have a look around and were fired on. The sergeant then swam back while his officer gave him covering fire, and once safely back, the sergeant organised covering fire while his company commander also swam to safety. All three men were awarded the Distinguished Service Cross for their exploits.

Further up river, the 10th Infantry moved into Montereau and established another bridgehead across the Seine, in the face of only light resistance.

The other armoured division of XX Corps, 7th Armoured, was assigned the task of creating yet another bridgehead at Melun, twenty-five miles from Paris. The two leading combat commands covered the ground to Melun with commendable speed, but when they tried to enter the town they were brought to an abrupt halt. The division commander, General Silvester, therefore turned his attention to a crossing at Tilly, downstream from Melun, and there a slender bridgehead was secured on 23rd August. The crossing was consolidated when engineers built a bridge on 24th August.

Thus the Seine was crossed on both sides of Paris, but by this time, events in the city were forcing the Allies to change their plans, and instead of the encircling and holding action they planned, it had become necessary to carry out an offensive action to take the city.

The plan for the liberation of Paris had been based on the need to avoid the obvious delay involved in capturing the city street by street in a long and costly action. The Allies had thought it feasible to surround the city and wait for the garrison to capitulate, while they went on beyond the Seine. Bringing the Germans in

Paris to an unnecessary military confrontation might, it was felt, prompt them to destroy the city. Indeed Hitler, on either 22nd or 23rd August, issued an order which made clear his intentions. He said that the loss of Paris would mean the loss of France, and that Paris must not fall into the hands of the enemy, except as a field of ruins.

That it did not ultimately do so was attributable largely to the actions and decisions of the garrison commander, General Dietrich von Choltitz. Choltitz had been given the mission of holding the city fortress, and had orders from Hitler to prevent the Allies crossing the Seine by pressing all troops into the front line, and by preparing to demolish all the bridges within the city, of which there were more than seventy. Hitler subsequently rescinded this last part of the order, on the grounds that the Germans themselves would need the bridges for their retreat behind the Seine.

To the eternal benefit of the civilised world, however, the question of the destruction of the city never arose. Choltitz was not the kind of man to countenance such a step and he later admitted that he was unwilling to endanger the lives of women and children. In any case, he was prevented from doing so by the development of circumstances, largely arising out of the changing role of the French Forces of the Interior (FFI) – the Resistance. As early as 18th August, encouraged by the progress of Allied troops on the continent, the Resistance movement had started to stir in Paris in a new and powerful way. On that day more than half the railway workers came out on strike, and on the following day they were joined by the armed French police force. Instead of an apparently obedient Parisian population, the Germans in the garrison were faced with public anti-German meetings, posters in the streets calling for insurrection, and at times even the appearance on the streets of armed members of the FFI. Choltitz was threatened with unrest which he was far too weakly equipped to control. When he failed to react to these minor irritants, the Resistance took even bolder steps, and small groups forcibly took over the main public buildings and police stations.

Fortunately, it was in everybody's interest to avoid a head-on clash. The Resistance members themselves were anxious not to precipitate the destruction of the city, and to avert reprisals against the civilian population, and they found an excellent 'go-between' with the Germans in the person of the Swedish consul, Raoul Nordling. Choltitz himself was prepared to make concessions and listen to Nordling for several reasons: he benefitted from an extended peace in the capital itself by being free to prepare the defences outside the city, and he also hoped that by maintaining the peace he could destroy the unity among the several factions within the Resistance, and play off one against the other, possibly even causing them to fight each other and destroy themselves.

Thus Nordling was able, on the evening of 19th August, to arrange a truce between the Germans and the Resistance, in the terms of which certain sections of the city were yielded to the Resistance, and others were to be left free for the unimpeded passage of German troops.

It was perhaps, in the last analysis, this apparent weakness on the part of Choltitz which set the Allied commanders thinking that they could take the city instead of bypassing it. The French generals, particularly, were anxious to restore French national pride with a liberated Paris, and they had a firm promise from the supreme commander that when the time came, the honour would be accorded to French troops, who had been included in the forces for Overlord specifically for that purpose. The one snag at this late stage was that when the Third and First Armies were at the gates of Paris, the French 2nd Armoured Division was still over a hundred miles away at Argentan. Now, however, the French were anxious to see their promise fulfilled, and on 21st August General Eisenhower received a letter from de Gaulle implying that if the Supreme Commander did not send troops to Paris at once, de Gaulle would do so himself. Eisenhower properly rejected the request, and there began a series of misunderstandings, mistakes, and acts of military insubordination in which the French not only proved a constant embarrassment to the Americans, but showed that their talents were infinitely more highly developed in the theatrical arts than in the martial ones.

The first instance occurred when Leclerc, acting without orders, decided to send a force of about 150 troops with light tanks armoured cars and personnel carriers towards the capital. His intention, it seems, was to make sure that if the Allies decided to enter Paris at least some Frenchmen would take part in the liberation. On the previous day, 20th August, General Hodges had turned down a request from Leclerc to send his division to Paris, and told him to stay put until he was ordered to move. General Gerow, V Corps commander, under whose command the French division now fell, received a curt note from Third Army headquarters asking what the French troops were doing outside their sector, and Gerow's reaction was equally abrupt. He sat down and wrote a note to Leclerc in his own handwriting, unequivocally setting out his position: 'I desire to make it clear to you that the 2nd Armoured Division (French) is under my command for all purposes and no part of it will be employed by you except in the execution of missions assigned by this headquarters.'

The French moves were not without their effect, however. They were one small part in a large volume of pressure which was being brought to bear to persuade Eisenhower to change his mind: de Gaulle had requested it; the French people wanted a liberated capital; even the Combined Chiefs of Staff had indicated that they had no objection to de Gaulle's entry into Paris. Most important, there were indications that the Germans were willing to abandon the city without much of a fight. Choltitz had told Nordling that he could not surrender the city to the FFI irregulars, and this was taken to indicate that he might be willing to turn the city over to the Allies after a nominal show of force. Further weight was added to the arguments when Resistance contacts reported that the city was ready to be taken over, and that the Germans defending it were relying largely on

Left: **Major-General Dietrich von Choltitz, Commander of the Paris garrison.** *Below:* **The FFI man makeshift barricades to help in the liberation of their city.** *Bottom:* **The popular Americans**

bluff. The situation was far from clear, but the balance of evidence and opinion was enough to sway Eisenhower. He decided to enter Paris.

The mission was assigned to General Gerow's V Corps, which had the French troops under its command. The corps also included, for the purpose of the liberation, the US 4th Infantry Division, an American cavalry reconnaissance group, and a British contingent, making a varied and truly Allied force for the task. Leclerc himself would thus liberate the city, but would do so under the direct leadership of General Gerow. Gerow paid particular attention to preparing detailed orders for the French, since they had already established a reputation for going whereever, and doing whatever, they pleased, regardless of their mission. But even minutely detailed orders were not enough. On the evening of 22nd August Gerow telephoned Leclerc and ordered him to start marching immediately: he started marching on the morning of 23rd.

The approach to Paris was by no means as easy as expected. On the western and southern approaches to the city, Choltitz had deployed some 20,000 troops, with tanks, anti-tank weapons, and artillery. Far from being ready to hand over the city to the Allies, he was determined, although anxious to prevent its wholesale destruction, to defend it around the perimeters with all his resources. When Leclerc learned of the strength of the defence in the Versailles/Rambouillet area, he decided, again contrary to orders, to divert the main weight of his attack from the west to the south. In fact his information was entirely erroneous, and the defence was strongest in precisely the area where he now intended to attack. In addition, his shift of axis placed his troops within the sector assigned to General Barton's 4th Division.

The Frenchmen attacked towards Paris at dawn on 24th August, and approached the city in two columns. The left column, under Colonel de Langlade, immediately ran into the German defences, and was held up for four hours in a fire fight which ended in the destruction of three out of eight German tanks. Having despatch-

ed that blockage, the column encountered an even more impenetrable barrier, in the thousands of French civilians who turned out to welcome their heroes, garland them with flowers, and ply them with wine and kisses. The problem was a serious one, and it was evening before the column could push on to the Pont de Sèvres.

The right hand column, under Colonel Billotte, faced even more serious opposition, this time entirely from the enemy. They were bogged down in the small villages outside the capital by a series of well sited strongpoints, and suffered heavy casualties. Out of seventy-one men killed and 246 wounded or missing in the battle to reach Paris, most casualties occurred on that day. However when darkness fell the defence evaporated. Choltitz ordered his troops to withdraw behind the Seine, and Billotte's column, aided by enthusiastic civilians who cleared the streets of the trees they had felled to hamper German mobility, encoutered no further resistance. By midnight they had reached the Hotel de Ville. On 25th August, Paris erupted into one enormous welcoming festival, as its people turned out to cheer and embrace the troops. By noon the 4th Division had reached Notre Dame, and the two French columns met at Rond Point des Champs Elysées. A third column of French troops, following Langlade, and under the command of Colonel Dio, encountered sharp resistance from Germans in some of the public buildings.

Despite the hopelessness of his situation, Choltitz refused to capitulate, even when Nordling conveyed to him an ultimatum from Billotte. In the end his headquarters, in the Hotel Meurice, were surrounded by French tanks. Fighting broke out, and the French burst into the hotel. Choltitz was taken prisoner.

Having arrived in their capital city, the French seemed to think the war was over. While the Americans set about the serious problems of holding and administering a great city, the French commander, Leclerc, chose to ignore such mundane affairs and settled down to the infinitely more important question of eating lunch. General Barton, commander of 4th Infantry Division, found him doing so at the

General de Gaulle returns in triumph to his city

Victory parade; the start of the pursuit

Préfecture de la Police, and Leclerc, annoyed at being distrubed, brusquely referred Barton to his headquarters at the Gare Montparnasse. Leclerc further put his undiplomatic foot in it when he had Choltitz brought to the Préfecture de la Police, and made him sign a formal declaration of capitulation, in the presence not of the Allies, but simply of himself and the Resistance leader. He claimed that the surrender was being accepted not on behalf of the Allied Expeditionary Force, but on behalf of the French Provisional Government.

The climax to the whole comic-opera episode came when General de Gaulle entered the city. There was no doubt about the strength of his support, and Gaullists were in firm control already of government and public affairs. De Gaulle appeared in Paris on 25th August, and the fervour of his welcome prompted him to lay on a parade to consolidate his position and demonstrate all round the weight of his power. While the French division constituted the main body of the parade, de Gaulle invited Gerow to take part by sending an officer and twenty men from each of the British and American forces to represent the Allies. Gerow's reply showed that he had not changed his opinion about Leclerc. He still faced the problems of clearing isolated Germans out of the city, for some had still not surrendered, and he wanted the city prepared to repulse a counterattack from the Germans either on land or from the air. He therefore ordered Leclerc to maintain contact and pursue the enemy. Leclerc replied that he had to devote some of his forces to the parade for the official entry of the head of state, and that this took precedence over his responsibilities to his military commander. In reply, he received another uncompromising letter from Gerow: 'You are operating under my direct command and will not accept orders from any other source. I understand you have been directed by General de Gaulle to parade your troops this afternoon at 1400 hours. You will disregard those orders and continue on the present mission assigned to you of clearing up all resistance in Paris and environs within your zone of action.'

'Your command will not participate in the parade this afternoon or at any other time except on orders signed by me personally.'

Leclerc finally resolved his divided loyalties with a direct appeal to de Gaulle, who, with rather more regard for sentiment than for military expediency, asked the Americans if, since he had given them Leclerc, he could not have him back for a moment.

157

The parade took place, on 26th August, and was accompanied by a certain amount of disorder and some shooting. It was obvious who was responsible, and Leclerc had to impound the weapons of his own troops. On the day of the parade, with the Frenchmen unarmed, there were still 2,000 Germans in the Bois de Boulogne, and it was fortunate for the French that they chose that afternoon not to strike back, but to walk out of the Bois and surrender.

General de Gaulle and his military commander, General Koenig, later recognised the extent of the problems they had created, and apologised, promising to comply in future with American orders. De Gaulle even recovered his diplomatic manners sufficiently to write to Eisenhower expressing his thanks for giving Leclerc the mission of liberating Paris.

To redress the balance of opinion, and remind the French that the Allies, who had lost so many good men on the beaches and in the battles of Normandy, were at least concerned in the campaign, Eisenhower laid on a second parade which would consist mostly of an American division in full combat array. The parade would also serve the useful purpose of getting the division through Paris and up to the front without it being entangled in the intractable Parisian traffic jams. While the British refused to take part in any of the celebrations, the parade was a great success, and Bradley, Gerow, de Gaulle, Koenig, and Leclerc reviewed it from an inverted Bailey bridge. But the jubilant population remained resolute in its notion that Paris had been liberated, virtually unaided, by the French Forces of the Interior within the city.

It may seem, looking back, as if the whole campaign had been fraught with bickering, nationalistic antagonism, and squabbling among commanders. In this last episode, certainly, the supreme commander and the American Corps commander appear to have had more trouble dealing with the French than they had in combating the Germans. The worst aspect of it all was that the French appeared to resent the Allies even taking part in the liberation. It was as if they wanted all the prestige for themselves. Even the extensive Allied relief supplies, which were still the city's only source of subsistence six weeks after the liberation, were not enough to dispel the bitterness and resentment.

But there had been other disputes and differences, which were to be exaggerated when the participants came to write down their memoirs after the end of the war. It might be thought that having won so mighty a victory the differences could be forgotten, but almost all the generals were persuaded, with greater or lesser degrees of encouragement, to record their feelings. Whether the differences were of real significance, or were merely legitimate expressions of opinion, more than usually vociferous because uttered in the heat of battle, may be judged by comparing them with the disputes which arise in other fields. Would, for example, fewer disagreements, fewer conflicts of judgment, be likely to arise in the boardroom of a vast international industrial complex? Would so many figures of such calibre, stature, and individual brilliance as the commanders in the field in Normandy be able to agree more than they on the merits of a single course of action?

On the other hand, the Allied Expeditionary Force was governed according to a strict and clear hierarchy of command, and it might be claimed that any dispute implied on the part of the subordinate officer a disinclination to accept and obey a military order. Yet again, it may have been simply their unreserved obedience to orders that led men, whose own judgment on military matters was seldom brought into doubt, to feel frustrated and thwarted when they were expected to carry out a campaign which did not conform exactly to the way they themselves would have had it carried out.

Over and above all the disputes and disagreements stood two figures. One was the Supreme Commander, General Eisenhower, whose administrative ability in welding together a team of different nationalities has been remarked in so many places, and by so many commentators qualified to judge, that it need not be further emphasised. The other was Montgomery, who was responsible for the ground plan in Normandy, but who so often allowed the confidence of his subordinates in him to lapse. Did he plan the campaign as well as could be expected? Whatever his merits as a general, he certainly laid himself open to criticism for his method of operating. The American commanders, particularly, resented his distant, even aloof, manner, his appearance of talking down to his subordinates, his practice of giving his plans out in the form of finalised orders, without so much as a gesture towards inviting them to contribute ideas. There was little wonder that enough pressure suddenly developed, when Bradley took over his army group, for Eisenhower to assume command of the ground forces, thus reducing Montgomery to only the same status as Bradley, and relieving him of the 'operational control' which he still carried.

But what of his success as a general? It is fair, in the circumstances, to let Montgomery himself be heard. In *Normandy to the Baltic*, his account of the campaign in Europe, he acknowledged the criticism, and took pains to illustrate the results of the battle in terms of hard facts. His view may not be impartial, but the facts themselves are not in dispute, and the reader can form his own opinion from them.

Montgomery states: 'The enemy losses in manpower were not far short of half a million men; 210,000 were prisoners in our hands and the figures for killed and wounded were estimated at about 240,000. Material losses were equally severe; some 3,500 guns and 1,500 tanks were captured or destroyed, together with a vast amount of mechanical transport, horse transport and equipment of all kinds.'

'A total of forty-three enemy divisions had either been eliminated or severely mauled, apart from the formations isolated in the Brittany ports and the Channel Islands. Of the Army, Corps, and Divisional Commanders, twenty had been killed or captured and two others wounded; the Supreme German Commander had been changed twice. The outstanding point about the Battle of Normandy is that it was fought exactly as planned before the invasion ...'

Montgomery then gives a table which illustrates how the plan to re-tain the main enemy strength on the eastern flank had worked. It shows that west of Caumont, between 15th June and 25th July, the number of Panzer divisions had gone up from nil to two, the number of tanks from seventy to 190, and the number of infantry battalions from sixty-three to eighty-five. By contrast, on the sector east of Caumont, the number of Panzer divisions had gone up from four to six, the number of tanks from 520 to 645, and the number of infantry battalions from forty-three to ninety-two. Thus the hard fighting on the eastern sector had so inhibited the Germans' freedom of action that they were unable to divert any greater resources to combat the threat of an American breakout, than they were to contain the British and Canadians. And with such comparatively weak forces arrayed against them, it is hardly a matter for astonishment that the American breakthrough was successful. Montgomery's greatest justification lies in the speed with which the Americans were able to move once the breakout had occurred. As Montgomery says: '... I had given D+90 as the target date for being lined up on the Seine, ... in fact the first crossing of the river was made on D+75. That there were critics who became despondent and lacking in confidence at a time when well laid plans for victory were maturing satisfactorily is understandable, because they could not be given, for obvious reasons, the basic design within which those plans were being executed.'

Whatever the quality of his generalship, the armies which had fought under Montgomery, to Montgomery's plan, now not only occupied Paris, the symbol of victory in the battle of France, but stood poised for a new effort which promised to bring the war to a speedy end. With the successful D-Day landings and a great victory in the Normandy campaign behind the Allies, and German resistance crumbling wherever it happened to make a stand, there were few pessimists in that late summer of 1944 who did not anticipate a fast and convincing pursuit into the heartland of Germany. But there were surprises in store yet.

Bibliography

The author is grateful to the following publishers for permission to quote certain passages in this work:
Collins, London, and Harper & Row, New York
The Struggle for Europe by Chester Wilmot
The Office of the Chief of Military History Department of the Army, Washington, DC *Breakout and Pursuit* by Martin Blumenson
Hutchinson, London, and Houghton Mifflin, Boston
Normandy to the Baltic by Field Marshal Montgomery of Alamein
The Ministry of National Defence, Ottawa. Canada
Canada's Battle in Normandy by Colonel C P Stacey

Breakout and Pursuit Martin Blumenson (Office of the Chief of Military History, Department of the Army, Washington DC)
The Struggle for Europe Chester Wilmot (Collins, London. Harper & Row, New York)
Normandy to the Baltic Field-Marshal Montgomery of Alamein (Hutchinson, London. Houghton Mifflin, Boston)
Canada's Battle In Normandy Colonel C P Stacey (Ministry of National Defence, Ottawa, Canada)
The Tanks Captain B H Liddell Hart (Cassell, London)
We Defended Normandy Lieutenant-General Hans Speidel (Herbert Jenkins, London)
A Soldier's Story General Omar Bradley (Eyre & Spottiswoode, London. Holt, New York)
War as I Knew It General George S Patton (Houghton Mifflin, Boston)